"Ambitious people don't always include the word *fulfillment* when they define success. But as Helen Krug von Nidda points out, that omission comes at a cost. *Closing the Fulfillment Gap* gives us a clear path from uncertainty to action, blending research and real-world stories to show how to navigate setbacks, reconnect with what matters, and build a career (and life!) that feels purposeful, sustainable, and fulfilling."

—Amy Shoenthal, *USA Today*
bestselling author of *The Setback Cycle*

"We don't live in a world of ladders and linear paths anymore. *Closing the Fulfillment Gap* dispenses with the leadership platitudes and invites us to look at work as it exists today: not as a balancing act, but as amorphous, shape-shifting, and deeply personal. With a keen understanding of the real challenges women face at work today, Helen offers a fresh, grounded approach to designing a work life that evolves and grows with you."

—Terri Trespicio, author of *Unfollow Your Passion: How to Create a Life That Matters to You*

"*Closing the Fulfillment Gap* is a thoughtful and practical guide for anyone questioning whether success alone is enough. Drawing on research, real stories, and her MOVE framework, Helen Krug von Nidda helps readers reconnect their work with what truly drives them. In a time when many professionals are rethinking the role work plays in their lives, this book offers a clear and actionable path toward building a career that is both successful and deeply fulfilling."

—Alim Dhanji, Chief Human Resources Officer
and EVP, Corporate Affairs, at TD SYNNEX

"In *Closing the Fulfillment Gap*, Dr. Helen Krug von Nidda offers a powerful, research-backed roadmap for redefining success on your own terms. This is the guide for anyone ready to move beyond chasing purpose and start building a life that truly feels aligned."

—Dr. Ella F. Washington, PhD,
bestselling author of *Unspoken*

"An essential guide for women ready to redefine success on their own terms and design the work life they truly want."

—Deepa Purushothaman, author of
The First, The Few, The Only

"If you've worked hard and done everything 'right,' yet still feel unsettled, this book is for you. Success doesn't automatically lead to meaning or fulfillment—Helen Krug von Nidda shows you how to align them thoughtfully and strategically."

—Dorie Clark, bestselling author of
The Long Game

Advance Praise for *Closing the Fulfillment Gap*

"For years, we've been told to find our purpose as if fulfillment were a single destination. In *Closing the Fulfillment Gap*, Helen Krug von Nidda offers a more humane and realistic alternative: fulfillment as alignment between our values, our work, and the season of life we're in. This book is a thoughtful guide to navigating nonlinear careers with clarity, agency, and intention."

—Anne-Laure Le Cunff,
author of *Tiny Experiments*

"*Closing the Fulfillment Gap* offers a clear and actionable roadmap for anyone striving to do meaningful work. Helen blends research, personal insight, and practical tools in a way that makes growth feel attainable rather than overwhelming. Readers will walk away with a deeper understanding of what fuels them and a framework they can return to as they continue leveling up."

—Dr. Ruth Gotian, Thinkers50 #1 Emerging Management Thinker in the World and bestselling author of *The Success Factor*, *Financial Times Guide to Mentoring*, and *Mentoring in Healthcare*

"Good people don't leave because they can't do the work. They leave when the work no longer fits their lives. In *Closing the Fulfillment Gap*, Helen Krug von Nidda offers a practical framework to address this challenge. Her MOVE model helps individuals realign how they work, while giving leaders a clearer path to sustain performance and growth."

—Brian Baker, Chief People Officer at Teneo

"*Closing the Fulfillment Gap* is a transformative guide for anyone ready to reclaim joy and purpose in their work life. Helen Krug von Nidda blends deep insight with practical tools that cut through the noise and get right to what matters. This book doesn't just inspire. It equips you to design the work life you truly want, with community at the center. A must-read for anyone seeking clarity, courage, and sustainable fulfillment in a world that asks so much of us."

—Cate Luzio, Founder and CEO of Luminary

"I've seen how often the pursuit of 'success' overshadows what truly brings fulfillment. In *Closing the Fulfillment Gap: How to Design the Work Life You Want*, Helen Krug von Nidda reframes fulfillment as an ongoing practice rooted in alignment, self-awareness, and intentional choice rather than titles or timelines. With empathy and practical frameworks, she empowers readers to reclaim agency, focus on what they can influence, and find meaning in both the small moments and the bigger moves along the way. This is a thoughtful, timely guide for anyone ready to define success on their own terms and close the fulfillment gap."

—Fran Hauser, keynote speaker, leadership expert, and bestselling author of *The Myth of the Nice Girl*

"Witty, wise, and deeply grounded in research, Helen delivers a standout guide to career and fulfillment."

—Sarah Young, founder of Zing Collaborative and author of *Expansive Impact: An Invitation to Lead in Everyday Moments*

Closing the Fulfillment Gap

How to Design the Work Life You Want

Helen Krug von Nidda

Post Hill Press

A POST HILL PRESS BOOK
ISBN: 979-8-89565-621-1
ISBN (eBook): 979-8-89565-622-8

Closing the Fulfillment Gap:
How to Design the Work Life You Want

Cover Design by Sheila Parr
Illustrations by Mina Yanci Ibis

Post Hill Press
New York • Nashville
posthillpress.com

Published in the United States of America
1 2 3 4 5 6 7 8 9 10

For those seeking clarity, alignment, and joy.
This book is for you.

"How we spend our days is,
of course, how we spend our lives."

ANNIE DILLARD, *The Writing Life*

CONTENTS

Introduction: The Heart of the Journey 13

PART I - "MINE" THE GAP: YOU ARE HERE

Discovering where you are and identifying what is missing

Chapter 1: The Fulfillment Gap: Understanding What's Missing 29

Chapter 2: What We Can Learn from Thrivers 49

Chapter 3: Make Your Move: Understanding the Framework 68

PART II - MOTIVATION: PROPELLING YOU FORWARD

Uncovering what drives you at your core

Chapter 4: Motivation: What Brings You Here? 81

Chapter 5: Values: Exploring Your Core 84

Chapter 6: Skills: Harnessing Your Strengths 96

Chapter 7: Recognition: Acknowledging Your Value 110

PART III - OPPORTUNITIES: MAXIMIZING MOMENTS

Creating pathways for growth

Chapter 8: Optimizing Opportunities............................ 127

Chapter 9: Accessing Your Networks 131

Chapter 10: Work Ecosystem: Optimizing Your Workplace Dynamics ... 150

Chapter 11: Your Mindset Is Your Greatest Asset ... 168

PART IV - VISION: WHERE DO YOU SEE YOURSELF?

Designing your future with intention and clarity

Chapter 12: Personal Vision ... 187

Chapter 13: Current Self: Who Am I? ... 189

Chapter 14: Becoming You: Your Future Self ... 202

Chapter 15: Your Active Learning Path ... 214

PART V - ENCOURAGING COMMUNITY: CULTIVATING YOUR CIRCLE OF CONNECTIONS

Building support systems that sustain your journey

Chapter 16: Never Go It Alone: Growing Together to Uplift and Empower ... 239

Chapter 17: Building "Movementum": Staying Actively Engaged on Your Path to Fulfillment ... 257

Staying Connected ... 261

Notes ... 263

Acknowledgments ... 283

About the Author ... 288

INTRODUCTION

THE HEART OF THE JOURNEY

It was 9 a.m. on a Saturday morning, the time when most people are playing catch-up with their lives, but Zara was one of five people in my coaching group at the IMD Business School in Switzerland, having elected to take an intensive weekend workshop as part of her MBA program.

Zara had recently embarked on an eighteen-month business degree, sacrificing weekends and evenings away from her husband and nine-year-old daughter, in the hopes that on the other side she'd have more professional opportunities to choose from within the sustainability industry where she'd worked for the last decade. Getting her MBA was transformational for her. But she was feeling downtrodden and dismayed because during her year-end review she didn't get the promotion she was expecting.

As she sat across from her boss, he thanked her profusely for her work and dedication, but it didn't take long before he told her there was no opportunity for a bigger role. Though it hadn't been explicitly said, her boss had previously indicated that an MBA was a natural path to promotion. But here she was with her advanced degree in hand, and he was telling her there was no room for growth at the company. His words felt like a betrayal.

A few months later, Zara realized something she hated to admit even to herself: She was truly unhappy and had lost her motivation for her work. She was on autopilot, feeling underutilized and uninspired by her job. She didn't have the opportunity to work on developing new projects, something she loved doing. She missed being in the driver's seat. And even worse, she was bored.

Purpose has been the word du jour for some time, offered up as the key to finding what will guide us to clarity in our lives. But while purpose has proven useful for some, a number of my coaching clients have found the concept too narrow a needle to thread. Author and neuroscientist Anne-Laure Le Cunff said in *Tiny Experiments,* "society has become obsessed with purpose driven careers, where the word *finding your purpose* has surged 700% over the past two decades." But what if *purpose* is too narrow an idea? What if finding one's purpose has many of us on a wild goose chase for our one true calling? Instead I think of our lives a lot like dating. There isn't one magical path, but many possibilities your life could take that would lead to fulfillment and joy.

Purpose has often been too focused on finding meaning in our *work* as if we can silo our lives into buckets: work and everything else. I specialize in coaching women to understand life as a puzzle. Each puzzle piece is a part of the larger picture. For some, the pieces might be health, work, and hobbies. For others, they might be family, love, and creative pursuits. The key is that everyone has a different vision for what they want, and that means that we are all continuously working toward completing our puzzle. Our picture might change along the way, which means looking for new puzzle pieces or switching some out. It's about letting our lives be in flow. What we want when we're twenty is likely very different than what we want when we're in our thirties, forties, and beyond. That's perfectly normal! Life isn't about marching orders. It's about making room for every version of ourselves.

Through my work with companies ranging from Morgan Stanley to Soho House to Nestlé to Sony Music to UN agencies worldwide, I have designed and led hundreds of coaching workshops across the globe in English and French to support women in centering their lives around fulfillment. Fulfillment is not about being a C-suite executive. It isn't necessarily about bigger paychecks or more prestigious titles or about climbing the career ladder either. Fulfillment is a feeling of satisfaction and well-being. It's about managing the unsatisfying work we all have to do with a sense of understanding that even the small stuff is part of the path that will lead you to a place of fulfillment. It's about creating and cultivating the life that's going to bring you the most joy. And it's what more and more women are seeking out.

My work focuses primarily on women because systemic barriers to career fulfillment often impact women differently. However, the framework and strategies in this book work for anyone seeking more fulfillment in their work life.

Even though there's been a surge in opportunities for many of us in the last fifty years, the mental and emotional pressure—and physical energy—of managing our lives has outpaced the returns. We are overwhelmed and exhausted. We feel dissatisfied and underappreciated. Where does this lead us? To more women opting out of the workplace. Quiet quitting. Staying stuck. Questioning society's definitions of success. Resigning themselves to the fact that they can't have it all.

But change always comes out of the ashes. In the last few years, we've seen a radical rethinking—a move toward personal *and* professional fulfillment. Many of us were raised by mothers who faced an opportunity gap in the '50s, '60s, and '70s. Today, we're facing a fulfillment gap, where despite the many advances that have been made across the globe, the systemic, organizational, and personal barriers to women's progress have left us wondering: How do we make the sustainable positive inroads to what we want for ourselves? In other words: How do we close our fulfillment gap?

In their seminal book *Intrinsic Motivation and Self-Determination in Human Behavior*, psychologists Edward Deci and Richard Ryan explored the concept of self-determination, revealing that individuals are inherently motivated by a drive to grow and find fulfillment. Deci and Ryan point out that achieving ongoing growth requires experiencing autonomy (the ability to make our own choices), competence (the ability to leverage skills we aspire to use), and connection with others (the ability to forge meaningful relationships). By nurturing this trifecta, we find ourselves leading fulfilling lives.

So, why is fulfillment so hard to find today?

There are lots of reasons. The global pandemic created a massive, unignorable ripple effect—women in the workforce were displaced, lost their jobs, or resigned as they struggled to balance their needs at home with the needs of their professional lives. Even for those who haven't left their roles yet, McKinsey's *Women in the Workplace* report found that

10 percent of women were considering jumping ship within the next two years compared to only 9 percent of men.

Why? Because women are more disillusioned than ever as they try to navigate in a system that doesn't cater to their needs. Catalyst and Aspen Institute studies highlight that for women of color there's a concrete ceiling that is even more impenetrable. We've seen time and again that women remain overworked and undervalued. And that finding a more positive work life is all but impossible for many. Even for those who aren't looking to move up at their companies and are happy in their current role, establishing a sense of belonging, pinpointing a community of cheerleaders, and determining a set of values and a vision for the future has been hard to find.

At a time when women should be taking advantage of remote work, finding new leadership opportunities, and pursuing personal projects and hobbies, we remain as frustrated as ever as workplaces scramble to figure out the new normal. And the fallout for women who are disengaged and unhappy is significant. In fact, if we don't feel fulfilled in our work lives, it becomes challenging to show up as our best selves in other important areas of our lives too.

Success and happiness have often been thought of as a ladder, but a large number of women have learned the climb isn't worth it. For many, success brings stress and senseless levels of anxiety that make it nearly impossible to want to stay the course or fully embrace a career path. It has become simply too hard to fit into the archaic work system where success is defined following a male prototype that we have to pretzel ourselves to fit into. While this dynamic is particularly challenging for women, a number of men are also finding that the traditional model of success no longer serves them. The rigid expectations of workplace norms also leave men struggling to fit into roles that no longer feel relevant and connected with today's aspirations for work and life.

A 2026 report by the Oliver Wyman Forum that surveyed three hundred thousand employees revealed that personal fulfillment is now the second workplace priority. Fulfillment can no longer be ignored. When you're not fulfilled it not only hurts you, but it affects your entire family and the larger society too.

A number of personal-growth books take you on a journey to revamp your whole life, pivoting to something totally new. But I believe that finding fulfillment is about making incremental shifts just as much as seismic ones. If you're a middle manager, how do you find fulfillment if you don't necessarily want a promotion? If you're a senior professional seeking new challenges without giving up your job title, what are some avenues to pursue? If you are working full-time but dream about exploring a side project, what are some options? If you've started a new job and realize you dislike it, how can you shift to a more fulfilling role? If you are returning to work after a parental leave, how do you re-engage with your team? And how do you identify an approach that allows you to find your footing and press on the gas at the same time?

We can't all throw out the baby with the bathwater when it comes to finding fulfillment. Many of us need our current jobs or don't have the financial safety net to take an extended time off to figure out what we want to do next. That's why I spend time in the following pages helping you explore what's possible within the constraints of your existing life. I talk about finding "pockets of play" or moments of movement within your days. *Wall Street Journal* reporter and editor Emily Bobrow wrote about how when she interviewed women across the country, including a Target cashier in Brooklyn, a Honduran immigrant with a beauty salon in Corinth, Texas, and an out-of-work professional-services executive in Nashville, Tennessee, they all told her that a fulfilling and even happy life doesn't mean that every moment is perfect. Many days are tough, but they also include moments of serving others, of human connection. Finding more joy within your current situation is part of the answer to a fulfilling life. It's about recalibrating, operating from a new perspective, owning your space, and paying attention to what you can influence. It's about increasing your awareness of the opportunities that you *can* pursue. Think of fulfillment like a pendulum, swinging back and forth depending on the season, the time of day, or how you're feeling at a particular moment.

The key is that *you* choose the energy and direction the pendulum swings. Dr. Sonja Lyubomirsky's research, particularly in *The How of Happiness* and *The Myths of Happiness,* has been foundational in shaping my perspective on personal growth. In these books, the Distinguished Professor of Psychology at the University of California, Riverside, talks about how 50 percent of our happiness is determined by our genes, while 40 percent is determined by our behavioral choices and 10 percent by our life circumstances. While her research has faced criticism by those who think she oversimplifies happiness, her core message remains powerful: The behaviors and thought patterns we cultivate significantly contribute to our well-being.

My HR journey began in recruitment, where I became captivated by the *why* behind people's career choices—what drew them to certain roles and how those choices shaped their identities. This curiosity blossomed into a passion for helping others connect the dots between what they do and who they are. My work has deepened my understanding of how career paths and personal identities intertwine across cultures.

I've taught at Stanford and Columbia Universities and coached at business schools including INSEAD and IMD, helping students and professionals alike connect with their strengths. I've also led team retreats, trainings, and coaching seminars in the private sector. And no matter where I'm working, my mission remains the same: to help individuals—especially women—embrace their potential.

Whether I'm doing a session with a startup founder, a middle manager at a finance company, or a C-suite executive at a private firm, it seems that everyone is searching for that feeling of well-being and satisfaction known as fulfillment, and they hit similar speed bumps and pain points along the way. Wherever I go, women tell me they are stuck without the tools to help them move toward action. Even with all the perceived choices and opportunities women have today, it's still challenging. Instead of pouring our energy and efforts into what we can control (that 40 percent), we obsess over whether our boss will give us the promotion we've worked so hard for or whether our client will renew our contract. Like Zara, we follow the path set out for us, and only when we hit an impasse—when other people's decisions don't match up with what we want for our lives—do we stop and take notice. Was Zara really unhappy with her job? Or did she only see how unfulfilled she was once her boss informed her that even with her MBA, she wouldn't get the role she yearned for?

Unfortunately, for most of us, we focus the majority of our time on what we can't control, which slows us down. We spend countless hours mired in self-doubt. My book will help you see that the roles, responsibilities, and relationships that *you* can shape are the heart of the journey.

To address the issues Zara and so many of the women I work with face, this book introduces the four building blocks of the MOVE framework that I developed from thousands of hours of client work on career and leadership development and from my doctoral research. It has helped shape my coaching with countless clients, and by the end of the book, my hope is that you will be able to use the framework to create a more joy-filled life too.

A few months into her period of deep dissatisfaction—and disconnected from the work she loved—Zara reached out to me for coaching. Through our work together with the MOVE framework, she began to shift her situation. It wasn't quick or easy, but by taking incremental steps, she created a work life that felt fulfilling. We will follow her journey throughout this book.

The MOVE building blocks—Motivation, Opportunities, Vision, and Encouraging Community—stem from the pitfalls I've seen clients fall into again and again. If you don't have the motivation or haven't identified the opportunities in front of you, closing the fulfillment gap will be farther out of reach. If you don't have a clear vision for what you want or don't have a community of supporters, it's much harder to stay on track. This framework was built with the barriers that most of us face in mind, and its proven strategies and activities help move you past common hurdles and deepen self-reflection along the way.

Here are the building blocks and their underlying categories:

- **Motivation:** Values, Skills, and Recognition.

- **Opportunities:** Access to Networks, Understanding Your Work Ecosystem, and Growth Mindset.

- **Vision:** Your Current Self, Your Active Learning Path, and Your Future Self.

- **Encouraging Community:** The supportive network of individuals who uplift and motivate you and form a bond of trust and belonging.

Think of the MOVE framework as a board game where you explore the strategies, options, and new ideas that move you closer to personal fulfillment. First you will learn how to get clear on your motivation, so you have a baseline understanding of who you are and where you are today. Then you will explore the opportunities that need attention and are ready to be surfaced. Next you will pivot to vision because understanding who you want to become—and what your future self looks and feels like—sets you up for the path ahead. And lastly, with motivation, opportunities, and vision identified, pinpointing your encouraging community is the final piece that provides you with foundational support. This model is tactical and reflective. As you learn how to MOVE, you'll see what needs the most attention in your life.

This book gives you permission to dedicate time to yourself. There may be unforeseen bends in the road, but how you accelerate into the curve may make all the difference. The idea is to press on the gas with intention and clarity, and importantly, with joy. You can read these pages on your own or if you prefer, gather a group of women and explore the activities together. The added benefit is that you have the support, encouragement, and feedback of a community, which plays a vital role in your personal and professional development. As you'll learn, community provides a space where individuals feel valued and supported; where shared stories create and strengthen bonds; and where there's an opportunity for accountability.

I've seen firsthand that there are so many different definitions of fulfillment. One employee's fulfillment is another's sense of failure. This book will show you how to define your own personal vision of fulfillment—and not just see it off in the distance but create a life that brings you in line with what you are wanting for yourself. It will help you identify what is getting in the way of a fulfilling life and offer a roadmap that will help you reassess and find the direction you've been looking for. It contains activities, practical advice, anecdotes, and case studies to meet and support you wherever you are on your journey. But it's important to note that fulfillment is not a quick fix or a Band-Aid for life's hiccups. Instead it's a long-term solution for what's ailing you whether you're stuck in an unfulfilling role, reentering the workforce, lost, undecided about what's next, or ready to make a small—or big—change.

Throughout this book, you'll find activities designed for pen and paper. There's something grounding about slowing down, writing by hand, and giving your thoughts room to unfold. At the same time, the ways we explore our lives and careers continue to evolve. Many people now turn to digital tools, including AI, as thinking partners—to brainstorm, to untangle a question, or to look at a situation from a new angle. Used with intention, these tools can add momentum to reflection and invite fresh perspectives.

PART I

"MINE" THE GAP: YOU ARE HERE

Discovering where you are and identifying what is missing

CHAPTER 1

THE FULFILLMENT GAP: UNDERSTANDING WHAT'S MISSING

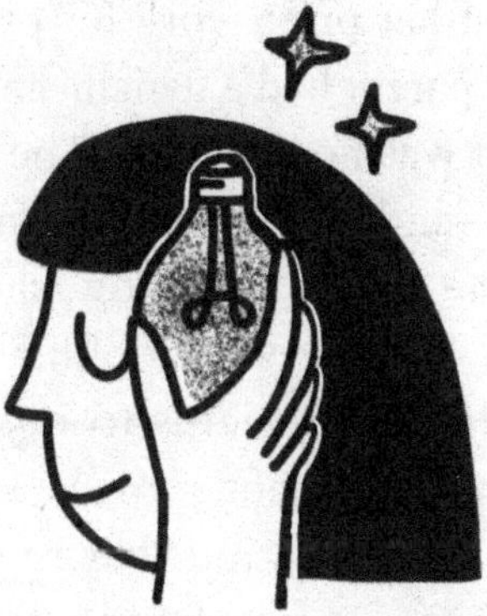

"Honestly, I don't have a purpose that I'm aware of. I'm just looking to do something that I at least enjoy working on," said my coaching client Yvonne on our introductory call where we explored working together and whether we might be a good fit.

This was what I refer to as our "shall we dance?" moment, and Yvonne cut right to the chase. "My friend suggested that 'purpose' might be a good place to start reflecting on what was next in my work life." She paused, waiting to see what I would say. When I smiled, she let it all hang out. "But the truth is that the idea of purpose is throwing me off. And giving me added stress."

I wasn't the least bit surprised.

Many of my clients tell me that rather than tapping into their curiosity around who they want to be in the world, *purpose* ramps up the pressure. Now Yvonne was in a bind, looking for clues that might give her a sense of what her purpose might be. She couldn't think of anything, though. As mother of two children under ten, being a parent was certainly a purpose, but her prior work for private-equity firms before she became a parent had a dynamism and drive that she loved, which she felt was now lacking. The mental energy her previous job took—and the money she made—gave her a sense of being on the right track. Now, she felt lost.

When we met, Yvonne was looking to return to the workforce after a four-year hiatus to raise her family, and she was deeply unhappy chasing jobs she knew she wouldn't find fulfilling. There was the job that required a two-hour commute, the job that was five days in person, the role that didn't pay a decent wage but had a great culture. Her priorities had changed, and none of them were right for her now. So, she steered clear in the hope of finding something more aligned with her aspirations.

But Yvonne had no idea anymore about what would help her feel fulfilled. Or rather, she had many ideas. To help her explore what these ideas might be, I reframed the conversation from "what does she want to *do*" to "what does *being* mean for her." One prompt that I use regularly with clients comes from the work of Dr. Richard Boyatzis, Distinguished University Professor at Case Western Reserve University and author of *Helping People Change*. It asks individuals to write down twenty-seven things they want to experience in their lives. Why twenty-seven? It's a number Dr. Boyatzis picked (he does encourage people to add more if they can) for pure intrigue, and I've found it works because the prompt inevitably gets people to scribble down a long list of things they are curious about in the world. These are clues. Clues as to what they may find fulfilling.

In a *Harvard Business Review* article, Stephen Friedman, organizational studies professor at the Schulich School of Business in Toronto, Canada, suggests that if we spend time focusing on the parts of our particular roles that we enjoy, or like, *that* can show us what we find fulfilling. In fact, the research backs up this idea: Working on something that brings feelings of contentment and satisfaction can in turn give meaning to life.

These days, it feels like contentment and satisfaction aren't enough for many of us. We instead want to feel a sense of permanent joy, which is unrealistic. Social media has perpetuated the illusion that everyone's lives are better than ours. Everyone else is taking a perfect vacation in Italy. Everyone else is living like a lifestyle guru. Everyone else is working at their dream job. That is certainly how Yvonne felt as she looked at her peers. Yet, if everyone is having such a good time, why did journalist Anne Marie Chaker write in the *Wall Street Journal* that even despite growing family policies and mental health services, women in the US remain less satisfied and more frustrated with their jobs than men? And, I would add, less satisfied in their personal lives, too.

In my conversations, I've found that there is often a simmering sense of impatience related to finding personal and professional fulfillment. But observing misalignment is only the first step in making a change. Once we acknowledge that something's amiss, the next step is arming ourselves with the patience and grace to embark on the exploratory journey of closing the fulfillment gap. The question so many of us forget to ask is this: *What do I want my life to look like?*

It's a question Yvonne was asking herself over and over. And while she didn't know what her answer was, she did know she was missing a sense of fulfillment. Yvonne is not alone. "*Fortune* magazine found that of the 108 women appearing on its list of top 50 most powerful women over the years, at least 20 chose to leave their high-powered jobs, most voluntarily, for lives that are less intense and more fulfilling," writes Lisa Belkin in *The New York Times*. My own research findings point to the same conclusion. Somehow achieving greater educational, political, and employment opportunities hasn't made us happier, probably because while those doors being open to us has meant more money, prestige, and power, that's not ultimately what women want. Or at least it's not the *only* thing women want.

> ” **Somehow achieving greater educational, political, and employment opportunities hasn't made us happier.**

Here's what closing the fulfillment gap could mean:

- Seeking an entirely different direction to your career
- Leaving a company for another organization in a similar field
- Recreating a role in the same organisation
- Deciding to become an entrepreneur
- Seeking to refocus on family

Despite attaining unprecedented levels of professional success, many women are still feeling like something is missing. And that missing puzzle piece is the fulfillment gap.

THE OPTIMAL CAREER JOURNEY

If you think about an optimal career journey, it has traditionally been viewed as linear, where individuals are promoted based on opportunity and merit. But the truth is that this career path has become a rarity.

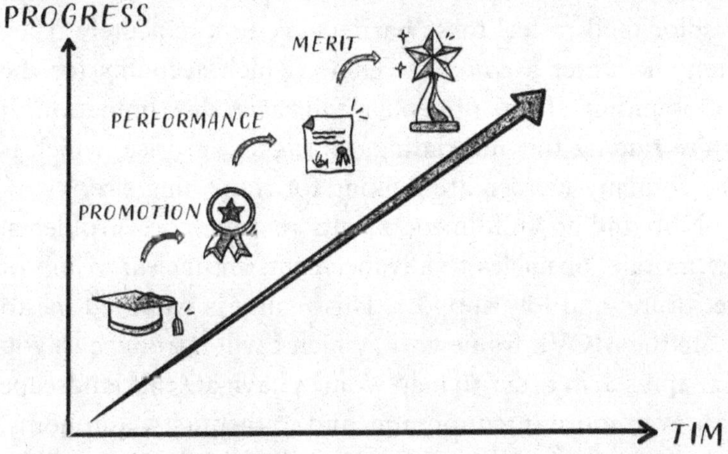

Today, people's careers are no longer a straight shot to the top. Rather they twist, turn, and evolve over time. The concept of "squiggly careers," a term coined by Helen Tupper and Sarah Ellis in their book *The Squiggly Career*, reflects how modern career paths are increasingly fluid, with lateral moves, career breaks, and reinventions becoming the norm. Our careers are landscapes, not ladders—and we are on a journey of exploration.

Research finds that for women in particular, the journey is often shaped by shifting priorities, personal values, and external circumstances. Women's career experience can feel like wading through mud while your boots are sinking into the ground. In fact, there's a term for that feeling: "sticky floor syndrome," which refers to the barriers women face—whether systemic, organizational, or personal—that keep us stuck. Even if women manage to overcome those barriers, they're still faced with the glass ceiling, the invisible barrier, which limits their access to senior roles. And women of color tend to feel these barriers even more acutely. They often encounter a *concrete* ceiling, which accounts for the compounding effects of gender and racial discrimination. If you're finding this infuriating, that is no surprise, which is why so many women are looking for something else.

Not finding fulfillment results in four core problems: low morale, obstacles to advancement, an unclear vision of the future, and low support. This reality is what led me to create the MOVE framework, which I will introduce to you in chapter 3, in order to help women navigate this landscape with even more intention and find authenticity, autonomy, and ultimately, fulfillment. By the end of this book, you'll be equipped with the tools to better understand what will bring fulfillment to your work life, bringing a shift from low morale to motivation, from encountering barriers to leveraging opportunities, from a murky and muddy road ahead to a clear vision for the future, from feeling excluded to being a part of an encouraging and supportive community.

I should also note that your lack of fulfillment is not because there is something wrong with *you*. Research confirms that across the globe women continue to face significant barriers and issues in their work lives. A McKinsey & Company 2024 report highlights the "broken rung" phenomenon, which keeps women from entering management positions. Women are less likely than men to be hired into entry-level roles, and women are also less likely to attain their first promotion, which leads to men significantly outnumbering women at the managerial level. Unsurprisingly, it's even worse for women of color, who represent only 7 percent of current C-suite positions—just a four-percentage-point increase since 2017.

> **Your lack of fulfillment is not because there is something wrong with *you*.**

This doesn't even account for the fact that women still shoulder a larger burden of unpaid caregiving responsibilities, exacerbated by the pandemic. Even when women get past the broken rung and land in management roles, Catalyst's research shows that they often face higher scrutiny, are less likely to have sponsors or advocates, and continue to be underrepresented in critical decision-making positions. Time and again I have observed women being sidelined and left to flounder.

THE JUGGLE STRUGGLE

There are numerous reasons both systemically and internally for why women are flailing. And to begin to understand them you need to know about what I call the Three *C's*. We are stuck in the **comparison trap**, we are at **capacity**, and we are overly **committed**.

> ❞ We are stuck in the **comparison trap**, we are at **capacity**, and we are overly **committed**.

Research consistently shows that women tend to underestimate their professional capabilities compared to their male counterparts, an issue that impacts their work-life exploration. There have been studies showing that women often require more evidence of their competence before putting themselves forward for opportunities, whereas men frequently pursue opportunities even when meeting fewer of the listed requirements. Even when we have more advanced degrees and deeper expertise, we tend to think we're not cutting it. That lack of confidence hurts other women too because we end up viewing each other from a place of our own shortcomings. We are tethered to our own trap.

It doesn't help that women often put themselves last. I see it every day, when women prioritize other people's needs—family, bosses—everyone else seems to get placed ahead of them. So, when women end up in a role, their professional priorities take up disproportionate amounts of time and energy, yet they don't drop the ball on their caretaking roles either, leaving them spent, exhausted, and stressed. Countless studies back up this finding, including *The Double-Bind Dilemma for Women in Leadership* (Catalyst, 2024) and OECD's 2021 report *Caregiving in Crisis*, which illustrate how women in the workplace experience higher demands and fewer resources than men, as well as having to bear the additional burden of unpaid work at home.

The supposed era of "having it all" creates a double-edged sword: We question ourselves or feel judged by others for not leaning in enough. We look at what others are doing and say, *I want that*. But we think to get there, we need to add more, whether going back to school, climbing the career ladder, or adding a new skill. We never subtract. It doesn't help that a recent *Harvard Business Review* article concluded that *busyness* has been dubbed the new social status. Busy people are perceived to be important, and so the downward spiral of adding to our to-do list worsens. I think the term *the juggle struggle* sums it up perfectly. If you're finding this infuriating, that's to be expected. This book is about giving you the tools to move forward and not waiting for the system to change.

DROP THE BALL

To counteract the juggle struggle there's recently been a trend in magazine articles telling women to let go. Books are adding to the chorus too. In *Why We Can't Sleep,* Ada Calhoun beautifully highlights the pressure cooker of pain women find themselves in from doing too much—which allows us to see what we might stop doing. In *Rest Is Resistance* Tricia Hersey reminds us how essential it is to rest to reclaim our humanity, sanity, and strength. And Tiffany Dufu's *Drop the Ball* shows us the dark side of attempting to do it all. The only way through, she says, is to allow ourselves to only take on what's most important and let the rest go. It is a case of having it all, but not all at once.

The pandemic accelerated the conversation about the disappointments and frustrations of work and life. For a while it seemed like rebuilding a new way of working was top of mind for companies. Covid-19 showed us that remote work, Zoom meetings, and even flexible schedules wouldn't reduce productivity. But now that the memories of the pandemic have receded, many companies have asked their employees to come back to the office and ramp up their hours again as if nothing has changed.

But all is not lost. In fact, I've seen more and more women saying no to ways of working that are detrimental to their well-being—and taking ownership of their careers in the process. More women are starting businesses on their own terms. More women are recognizing that slow and steady really does win the race. Only when we close the fulfillment gap will we see the kind of human-centered workplaces and lives that we have dreamed about.

In their book, *Build the Life You Want: The Art and Science of Getting Happier,*

> Arthur C. Brooks and Oprah Winfrey define happiness as needing three elements:
>
> - Positive everyday experiences
> - Satisfaction, which consists of achieving intentions and feeling competent
> - Meaning or serving something larger than yourself

Whereas fulfillment is a state of prolonged contentment, happiness is more immediate—for example, meeting my best friend for a hot chocolate makes me happy. Momentary pleasures can bring happiness, while fulfillment comes from the sense that our actions and life choices align with a greater sense of growth and satisfaction. This creates a deeper sense of contentment that persists even through life's inevitable challenges. All of us will be pulled toward disruption and dissatisfaction. Closing the fulfillment gap means working to ensure things aren't happening *to* us, but that we are active participants in our own lives. Fulfillment is *contentment in a cup.* We each have a unique-sized cup to fill.

> Fulfillment is the feeling of well-being and ease you experience when you are in alignment with your intentions and your expectations.

When things aren't going well in our lives, we are in misalignment with what we desire and are prone to focusing on negative experiences. Research confirms that we tend to have a negativity bias, meaning that negative emotions have a stronger pull on us than positive emotions. That's because our brains are wired for survival, focusing on potential threats and negative outcomes to keep us safe. Experiences that are unfamiliar typically activate negative emotions.

So, how do we move toward more positive emotions, and, in turn, more fulfillment? By creating more opportunities for five research-backed experiences that have been proven to positively enhance emotions: mindfulness (like reciting a prayer or practicing tai chi), compassion (such as volunteering), hope (thinking positively about the future), playfulness, and walking in nature. Each activity helps shift the brain to a positive state that awakens personal growth and transformation.

Ironically, working through a challenging situation can also bring about a sense of fulfillment. For example, when we study for an exam, train for a marathon, or do something else where a lot of effort is required, the process itself can result in feeling fulfilled. Closing the fulfillment gap means intentionally doing things that are hard, that stir up our fears and give us the opportunity to prove ourselves. The MOVE framework will help you spend more time in that fulfillment zone.

In our quest for contentment, we often place a lot of pressure on our work life to fulfill all of our needs. Yet studies show that expanding our sources of fulfillment beyond work can significantly enhance overall life satisfaction. A number of cultures, for example, embrace this balanced approach; Mediterranean countries practice "la dolce vita," finding joy in savoring daily pleasures and meaningful connections, while Scandinavian countries embrace "friluftsliv," the celebration of outdoor life and connection with nature.

" Mediterranean countries practice "la dolce vita," finding joy in savoring daily pleasures and meaningful connections, while Scandinavian countries embrace "friluftsliv," the celebration of outdoor life and connection with nature.

Engaging in non-work-related activities is not only essential but encouraged. But psychologist Dr. Tal Ben-Shahar's concept of the "arrival fallacy" reminds us that achieving a distant goal like finally getting that corner office, earning a specific salary or winning a marathon often leads to fleeting satisfaction. True fulfillment exists not so much in the end goal but in the smaller, meaningful moments experienced along the way.

Participating in leisure activities also helps. Volunteering at a local shelter, joining a running group, taking that dance class you've been considering, joining a community garden, or dedicating time to creative pursuits can bridge that gap that work alone cannot fill. These actions meet your desires for autonomy, creativity, relationships, and by default make your work life better because these explorations are a *part of* what makes you fulfilled rather than *apart from* your work life. By diversifying our sources of contentment, we create a more resilient foundation for fulfillment that doesn't depend solely on our professional identity but is, rather, a complement to it.

Each moment of fulfillment—whether writing at dawn or sharing a meal—emerges from cultivating a natural flow of experiences rather than constantly shooting for the stars. Figuring out your own version will help guide you.

But don't fill up your plate too much in search of that elusive feeling of fulfillment. It's important to note that we need to protect our time so that these moments can unfold.

> **But don't fill up your plate too much in search of that elusive feeling of fulfillment.**

Protecting our time doesn't only mean clearing our calendar. It also means carving out a space conducive to exploration and being intentional about our mindset. Are you coming to this work grudgingly, excitedly, or with apprehension? What do you need in place before you set yourself up for success? When are you primed to do your best work?

Having your own space for exploration and creativity helps. My writing space is always our living room table (though I have a study, I prefer to be in the living room, which is one of the more colorful spaces in our home). Our table is a beautiful, long dark wood table, and I sit gazing out at the gingko tree in our shared courtyard. I always bring my computer, my favorite coaster made up of yarn of all colors, and surround myself with a few colorful cushions. But most importantly, I need soft instrumental music, jazz, or classical, throughout my writing time. I need absolute focus and also tunes I won't be tempted to sing along to while I work, so that is why I love having instrumental music playing in the background.

Before you even dive into this book, have you taken the time to prime your surroundings so you're ready to explore? Look at your immediate environment, what sounds are you hearing? What are you sensing, seeing, and feeling? What is needed for you to embark on this personal journey? Have you made space for dedicated, uninterrupted time?

This isn't about chasing permanent happiness or achieving specific goals (remember the arrival fallacy), but rather about cultivating awareness of when you're most aligned with yourself and deliberately choosing to return to that space. The more familiar you become with your motivations, values, and vision, the more naturally fulfillment flows from your daily experiences. And the easier it becomes to design the work life that works for you.

Part of creating the work life you want is also about recognizing what pulls you off-center, so that you can better understand what demands your attention and energy. Let's explore what's currently missing from your life in preventing you from achieving fulfillment with this simple assessment, which I call "Mine the Gap." The goal of this activity is to help you identify areas of misalignment in your work life by observing and assessing your current level of satisfaction.

ACTIVITY: MINE THE GAP

Step 1: Rate Your Satisfaction

On a scale of 1 to 10 (1 being *not satisfied at all,* 10 being *fully satisfied*), rate your current level of satisfaction in the following areas:

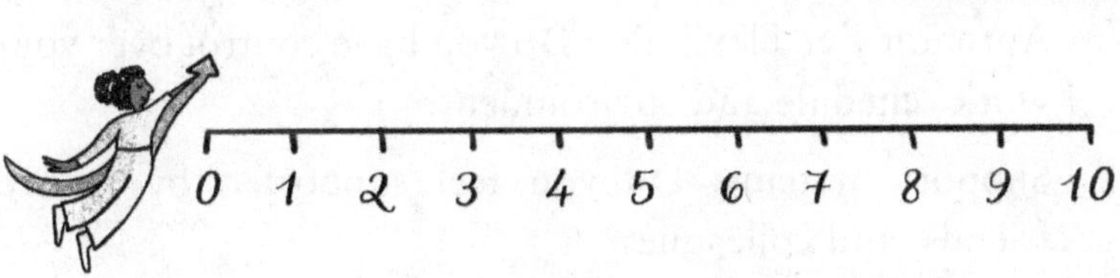

Professional Fulfillment

Work Satisfaction: How satisfied are you with your current job or career path?

Opportunities for Growth: Do you have clear paths for growth in your career?

Alignment with Values: Does your work reflect your personal values and beliefs?

Recognition and Validation: Do you feel your contributions are acknowledged and valued?

Personal Fulfillment

Meaningful Relationships: Are your relationships with family, friends, or significant others fulfilling?

Personal Growth: Are your learning experiences helping you grow personally?

Emotional Well-Being: How well do you manage stress and emotions?

Connection to Projects: Are you engaging in activities that bring you joy outside of work?

Work-Life Integration

Work-Life Harmony: Are you effectively balancing professional and personal commitments?

Autonomy & Flexibility: Do you have control over your work schedule and environment?

Support Systems: Do you feel supported by family, friends, and colleagues?

Boundaries: Are you able to set and maintain boundaries between your work and personal life?

Step 2: Reflect and Write

Circle any areas where you gave yourself a rating of 6 or below. These circled areas represent gaps in your current fulfillment.

For each area you circled, reflect on the following questions:

What may be contributing to low satisfaction in this area?

How does this gap affect your overall well-being?

What are the common themes or patterns across the areas where you rated yourself low?

How do these gaps make you feel?

What else are you observing?

Generally, how far off center are you?

If your ratings are mostly above 6:

This is a sign that you are already experiencing a high degree of fulfillment in areas of your life and that asking yourself the following questions might help you maintain this level of joy.

- What am I doing that already supports these higher ratings and how can I continue to nurture them?
- How can I leverage the areas I see as strengths to create momentum in other areas of my life?
- Are there any signs that I need to pay attention to in order to avoid any future dips?

This is your opportunity to *tend to your garden* as it were, pruning and protecting what is already in bloom.

This activity is meant to help you step back and identify what fulfillment means to you so that you understand your baseline and can mine your gap. It's also about recognizing where you're thriving. As you move forward, you'll have the opportunity to revisit these insights and explore next steps in the chapters that follow. For now, take a moment to sit with your reflections—this is just the beginning of uncovering what truly matters to you.

While the Mine the Gap activity helps you understand where you are today, Twenty-Seven Experiences invites you to focus on future possibilities, explore your aspirations, discover what matters to you, and signpost your journey ahead. This shift from present awareness to future paths highlights the gap between what's missing and what direction you might want to explore.

ACTIVITY: TWENTY-SEVEN EXPERIENCES

Step 1: Make Your List

Take ten minutes to write down twenty-seven things you want to experience in this lifetime, ideally on separate Post-its so that you can move them around. The point is to do it quickly without overthinking it.

1

2

3

4

5

6

7

8

9

10

11

12

13

14

15

16

17

18

19

20

21

22

23

24

25

26

27

Step 2: Find Your Themes

Once complete, group your list of Twenty-Seven Experiences into themes (e.g. travel, leadership):

YOUR THEMES

What themes emerge from your list?

What are you learning about what matters to you?

What surprises you about your choices?

What, if anything, seems absent from your list?

What else?

By understanding both where you stand and what you wish to experience, you can begin to bridge your fulfillment gap intentionally. Together, these exercises create self-awareness about where you stand today while simultaneously illuminating the path toward what you wish to experience in the future.

Now that you've gotten an overview of what fulfillment is and where you are at present, the following chapters will introduce the framework for closing this gap. You'll learn specific strategies to build upon the insights you gain along the way, no matter what stage or phase of your career you are in. Our focus, interests, and needs shift over time, and with people having longer career journeys than at any other moment in history, it's more important than ever to have the tools to design the work life you want—and at the end of the day feel fulfilled.

CHAPTER 2

WHAT WE CAN LEARN FROM THRIVERS

Sydney had a twinkle in her eye—a tiny diamond on my Zoom screen. I was taking notes as fast as I could. We had been in conversation for a good twenty minutes exploring how she had arrived at the sweet spot of work *and* joy and, most importantly, what had been the turning point. Sydney had worked eighty-hour weeks for as long as she could remember, she was usually on a long-haul flight each month, juggling her teams spread across the globe, leaping through time zones. She excelled at what she did, which meant she was being asked to do more. Based out of New York, she was also tasked with leading teams in Asia who had not been informed of her mandate. Instead of welcoming her into the fold, they stood in the way of her accomplishing any tasks. This, she told me, was a classic move on the company's part: minimal communication and disregard for cultural nuances. Continuous travel and endless communications hurdles took their toll. She was deeply frustrated and frazzled.

Unsurprisingly, Sydney experienced burnout at her job. Not only that, but she was bewildered at how she and her husband had managed to stay connected throughout those years. "Showing emotion was weak," Sydney said as she explained her former work environment. "My company was mostly male-dominated, and I just no longer wanted to be a part of that system."

As she explored her options, Sydney decided to work with a coach to identify what she wanted out of her career going forward. Ultimately, she chose to step away, thoughtfully and at her own pace.

"It was about living more authentically and being true to myself," she said, "and at the same time finding something that would motivate me again." But what would motivate her was a mystery. When I asked Sydney what she had been looking for, all she could tell me was that she wanted a career that had "some meaning in it."

That was a good place to start.

"You have to take a massive risk on yourself," was how Chloe jumpstarted our conversation. Chloe was a highly successful banker, but she was starting to think about her next move. Did she want a lateral, in-house role? Should she move to a competitor? Or should she seek yet another promotion at her same company?

She wasn't short of options.

But when she quieted down the *shoulds,* those persnickety expectations that had ruled most of her life, she knew there was only one way forward: refocusing her energy on helping professional women re-enter the workforce. She wanted to start a community for women—and not just an online option, but an in-person space where women could gather to collaborate and connect. Driven, focused, and unapologetic are the three words I would use to describe Chloe.

After returning from a women's event where she was yet again bombarded by women talking about the challenges they faced, she went home and wrote a business plan laying out what she envisioned. It took her two weeks to form that vision. A physical and digital space that would give women the community and connection to help them feel less alone and more in charge of their lives. "I knew that I was the right person to lead something like this," she told me, "and that I could have a real impact." Literally nine months later, Chloe opened the physical doors to her in-person community space.

Reka, a mom of three, almost immediately began reflecting on the consequences of constantly putting others' needs before her own when we met. Her lack of self-care changed her perception of who she was, which made her miserable at work and in her personal life. She stopped doing small things that made her feel like herself: her morning coffee routine, wearing her favorite jewelry.

"I didn't realize how much I was prioritizing other people's ideas about me above my own," she told me matter-of-factly. Once she had that revelation, she knew she needed to stop taking in negative feedback from others and start listening to those who really appreciated what she had to offer. She signed up for a class on mindset to learn "a different way of being so that I could get a different result." It was the reboot she needed.

Ultimately, she stayed at her corporate job, but she also joined a community of writers which, as she put it, propelled her creativity and catapulted her to become more in tune with the person she wanted to be. Instead of allowing others to shape her perception of herself, she found a way to break that pattern by taking a chance on trying something different to shift her perspective.

Sydney, Chloe, and Reka took three very different paths to joy. I think of them as *thrivers:* individuals who actively and intentionally work to close their fulfillment gap.

Thrivers take their work life into their own hands in both big and small ways. It's not about living happily ever after every single day, but through focused attention and setting their sights on choices within their control, they have the opportunity to find fulfillment more often and in more areas of their life.

My goal in speaking with thrivers was to find out what ignited their search toward greater fulfillment. What was the moment when they decided they needed more fulfillment in their lives? What was the catalyst for making real change? And what helped them stick with it once they saw the path in front of them?

WHAT IGNITES THRIVERS

As I spoke to more thrivers, I realized that what motivates them boils down to three common elements that I call the Three *R's*: a clear awareness of the level of *risk* they felt comfortable with, understanding of the impact of their choices on their *relationships,* and a sense of the *rhythm* of change they were prepared to experience.

The Three *R's*:

1. A clear awareness of the level of *risk* they felt comfortable with.
2. An understanding of the impact of their choices on their *relationships.*
3. A sense of the *rhythm* of change they were prepared to experience.

CHLOE'S THREE *R's*

Risk

Chloe had a successful career and was financially able to take on a high level of risk when it came to her career pivot. Having been in banking her whole life, she was extremely comfortable exploring a variety of work options because she was financially secure and knew that even when the waves were choppy she would make it safely to shore.

Relationships

Chloe immediately surrounded herself with people who could be a support system, including her partner who had her back every step of the way. She knew that her relationships weren't going anywhere and that she could lean on them as needed.

Rhythm

Having been used to working insane banking hours, Chloe was equipped to continue at that same pace. She also dealt with constant disruption having worked globally in different banking roles. Her work ethic and comfortability with change had already prepared her for what was to come.

SYDNEY'S THREE *R's*

Risk

Sydney, who was a few years away from retirement, knew she could handle a certain level of risk if her coaching practice didn't pan out. She wasn't prepared to retire altogether, but she was prepared to start a coaching certification alongside her full-time job. Once she had a sturdy plan, she felt ready to resign.

Relationships

Sydney took stock of the impact of her decision on her spouse. Being self-employed meant she would enjoy far more quality time with her partner, something he told her he'd longed for.

Rhythm

A coaching practice would also mean less travel for Sydney and a more predictable pace, a rhythm she could truly appreciate.

REKA'S THREE *R's*

Risk

Reka had absolutely no interest in taking any professional risks whatsoever. Not only could she not afford to contemplate a change, given she had a partner, three children, and a dog, but any decision she made would have too much of a ripple effect on the family. Her approach was different. Knowing she couldn't leave her current job, though it wasn't giving her much satisfaction, she chose to enroll in evening classes. That was minimal risk, and the "mindset" class she picked was affordable. Plus, her family were the recipients of her newfound upbeat mood.

Relationships

Reka's children were just entering their teenage years, and she knew that any disruption to her daytime schedule would add to the turmoil of a full household given that her husband had a fairly long commute to the office. Risking her relationship with her kids or her husband wasn't something Reka was willing to do.

Rhythm

She was pleased with the setup they had, child-care needs covered and most aspects working like clockwork. The last thing she had energy for was disrupting a household. Just like a driver, she had her eye on the road ahead. Taking an evening class once a week was a way to start making space for her own exploration. It was the beginning of her personal quest to find more joy—and it led her to join a community of writers who met virtually: another rhythm that suited her exploration.

The three women identified fulfillment in unique ways, which dictated their approach. Chloe is what I call a **Venturer**, someone who made strategic use of her work relationships and circles of influence to propel her forward. Sydney is what I call a **Seeker** because she's on a journey of self-discovery. And Reka is a **Navigator** because she prioritizes relationships, carefully considering the repercussions of any decision she makes on the people closest to her.

The Three *R's* will help you assess what's *possible* for you right now. Can you tolerate high risk, or do you need stability? Will your relationships support a big change, or do you need to tread more carefully? What rhythm of change feels sustainable? But the Three *R's* only tell you about your constraints and circumstances. They don't tell you what's *driving* you toward change in the first place. This is where your thriver type comes in.

Your thriver type—whether you're a Venturer, Seeker, or Navigator—reveals your underlying motivation. It's the *why* beneath your desire for more fulfillment. And knowing your why helps you choose the right path forward. These are not rigid categories but they are tendencies.

VENTURERS

Venturers are the ones who are the most open to making life-altering professional transitions. Think of Chloe, who attended a women's networking event and became so dismayed at women's inability to find professional support to reenter the workforce that she had a business plan written in two weeks and was ready for action. Similarly, Edina, a successful partner in a law firm, resigned from her job a few days after reading Parker Palmer's book *Let Your Life Speak: Listening for the Voice of Vocation.* Palmer's words challenged her thinking, which led her to start a nonprofit for victims of domestic violence. Venturers are powered by challenge, decisiveness, and commitment to their personal vision, which helps them to leverage their capabilities to create bold, visible impact.

Characteristics of Venturers:

- High tolerance for risk and uncertainty
- Strategic network building and leveraging of relationships
- Clear vision of their goals
- Learning from failure and setbacks as fuel for iteration
- Centered on achievement, growth and impact

Venturers are typically, albeit not always, accomplished senior-level executives who have a high level of visibility within their respective organizations. They work in high-pressure environments and are accustomed to, and driven by, working under challenging conditions. Their decisions to act on their personal vision are due to their high level of self-confidence and their ability to leverage their networks as well as their mentors. Venturers closed their fulfillment gap because they not only dared to dream, but acted upon their dreams in bold and ambitious ways.

> **Venturers closed their fulfillment gap because they not only dared to dream, but acted upon their dreams in bold and ambitious ways.**

SEEKERS

Seekers arrive at their need for personal fulfillment through a journey of introspection. They experience fulfillment by aligning their actions with deep values and contributing to something meaningful beyond themselves (as was the case for Sydney). Seekers are "formal learning junkies" who view skill development as both personal evolution and preparation for greater impact. They are keen to invest in capabilities that align with their purpose. I observed that Seekers experience deep dissatisfaction when their work conflicts with their values, often citing "corporate culture burnout" as a catalyst for change.

Characteristics of Seekers:

- Strong reliance on intuition for guidance and decision-making
- Medium tolerance for risk
- Active self-reflection and personal development
- Identity-focused mindset
- Values focused on meaning and contribution

Seekers are enthusiastic and avid learners who view skill development as both personal evolution and preparation for greater public impact. Seekers give themselves the opportunity to think things through and take the time in their search for more meaningful lives.

> **Seekers give themselves the opportunity to think things through and take the time in their search for more meaningful lives.**

NAVIGATORS

Navigators value balance and many prioritize family over their professional lives. They often develop "portfolio skills" that serve them in professional settings, parenting, community involvement, and personal interests. Think of Reka, who couldn't afford to upend her family's routine but still found a way to carve out space for her own growth. Navigators are powered by intention and a deep awareness of how their choices ripple outward, which allows them to create meaningful progress without sacrificing what matters most to them.

Characteristics of Navigators:

- High value on flexibility
- Family and community focused
- Motivated by learning that expands skills across multiple life domains
- Lower tolerance for risk, preferring steady and incremental change
- Identity rooted in multiple life roles, not just professional ones

They are often, though not always, individuals juggling multiple significant roles—professional, parent, partner, community member. Navigators close their fulfillment gap by making intentional choices that keep their own growth and the needs of those around them in view.

Navigators close their fulfillment gap by making intentional choices that keep their own growth and the needs of those around them in view.

WHICH DRIVE HELPS YOU THRIVE?

Understanding your motivation pattern isn't about tattooing it, as it's not permanent, but having a sense of your current driver is a helpful starting point.

Just like Sydney, who found herself yearning for deeper meaning, or Chloe, who wanted to take on a new challenge, having an idea of what motivates you will set you up for the road ahead. You might be looking to identify better work-life harmony or perhaps are hoping for ways to elevate your position within an organization. No matter what path lies ahead, an understanding of what drives you will help set the stage. The following quiz will help you identify your current thriver type. There are no wrong answers. It's an opportunity to find what motivates you right now.

ACTIVITY: THE THRIVE QUIZ

A reflection tool to help you understand what is currently driving your motivation and sense of fulfillment at work. This is not a personality test, and there are no right or wrong results.

Instructions

Rate each statement from 1–5 based on how much it describes you right now.

1 = Not like me at all

5 = Very much like me

(Don't worry about the letters in parentheses—they're just for scoring later.)

The Quiz

1. I feel energized by bold action and strategic opportunities. (V) 1 2 3 4 5
2. I seek learning opportunities that help me discover what I may want next. (S) 1 2 3 4 5
3. I value experimentation and flexibility over rapid advancement. (N) 1 2 3 4 5
4. I actively seek visible accomplishments and network strategically. (V) 1 2 3 4 5
5. I rely heavily on intuition for guidance in career decisions. (S) 1 2 3 4 5

6. I make career decisions with my broader responsibilities in mind. (N) 1 2 3 4 5
7. I have high tolerance for risk when I see strategic opportunities. (V) 1 2 3 4 5
8. I prioritize work that aligns with my core beliefs and values. (S) 1 2 3 4 5
9. I want to be valued for who I am beyond my professional title. (N) 1 2 3 4 5
10. I choose skills that position me for bigger opportunities or roles. (V) 1 2 3 4 5
11. I feel dissatisfied when work conflicts with my values. (S) 1 2 3 4 5
12. I prefer a sustainable pace that supports the other parts of my life. (N) 1 2 3 4 5
13. I leverage my skills to create bold, visible impact. (V) 1 2 3 4 5
14. I view skill development as personal and professional evolution. (S) 1 2 3 4 5
15. I prioritize both work progress and personal wellbeing. (N) 1 2 3 4 5

Scoring

Add up your scores for each category:

V (Venturer): Questions 1, 4, 7, 10, 13

S (Seeker): Questions 2, 5, 8, 11, 14

N (Navigator): Questions 3, 6, 9, 12, 15

How to Interpret Your Results

Your result describes what is currently fueling your motivation and sense of fulfillment in this season of your life. These drivers change over time as responsibilities, roles and relationships evolve.

Use the guidelines below to make sense of your scores:

- Your highest score: your primary driver right now
- Your second-highest score: a secondary pull or important influence
- If two scores are within 3 points, you are likely in a transition between drivers
- If none of your scores stand out clearly, it often means your priorities are actively shifting

When Two Drivers Are Rated High

Many people score highly in two categories. This often signals tension—the place where growth and important decisions emerge.

Examples:

- Venturer plus Navigator: ambition versus balance
- Seeker plus Venturer: meaning versus momentum
- Seeker plus Navigator: meaning versus stability

Noticing this tension can explain why work feels effortful or draining even when things appear to be working from the outside.

Your Current Driver

Venturer

You are currently drawn to fulfillment through challenge, momentum, and visible impact.

Common strengths:

- High tolerance for risk and uncertainty
- Strategic networking and relationship leverage
- Drive for growth and influence

Watch for these patterns when you're out of alignment:

- Ignoring exhaustion or personal limits
- Measuring worth only through achievement
- Staying in constant acceleration mode

Seeker

You are currently drawn to fulfillment through meaning, authenticity, and personal growth.

Common strengths:

- Sensitivity to what feels meaningful and aligned
- Deep self-reflection
- Commitment to learning

Watch for these patterns when you're out of alignment:

- Over-preparing and under-deciding
- Staying in misaligned environments too long
- Confusing discomfort with failure

Navigator

You are currently drawn to fulfillment through intentional choices, integration, and meaningful progress.

Common strengths:

- Strong sense of priorities
- Flexibility and adaptability
- Ability to manage multiple roles

Watch for these patterns when you're out of alignment:

- Delaying change in the name of stability
- Becoming less visible at work than you intend
- Carrying more than your fair share quietly

Using Your Result as a Compass

If your primary driver is Venturer, ask yourself:

- Where do I need challenge right now to feel engaged?
- What kind of impact do I want to be known for?
- What support would make bold moves sustainable?

If your primary driver is Seeker, ask yourself:

- What values am I no longer willing to compromise?
- What learning or growth would feel most meaningful right now?
- Where am I staying comfortable instead of aligned?

If your primary driver is Navigator, ask yourself:

- What does balance actually mean for me right now?
- Where do I want flexibility without disappearing?
- What small experiments would feel safe but meaningful?

This quiz is not meant to prescribe a career move. You might recognize elements of all three drivers in yourself, but one typically stands out when you're seeking greater fulfillment at work. This reflection serves as a compass, pointing you toward areas of exploration.

It is designed to help you notice patterns, name what matters now, and reduce the friction between how you live, work, and show up each day. You can revisit this quiz whenever your circumstances change.

Key Points:

- **Monitor Your Motivation:** Thriver types reveal the different motivations for fulfillment. Understanding what type drives you helps you to identify what needs attention.
- **Be Bold:** Thrivers take bold action and don't wait for permission.
- **Assess Your Comfort Level:** The Three *R's* help you determine your tolerance for risk, the impact on your relationships, and the rhythm of change that works for you.

- **Nothing is Permanent:** Your thriver type is not permanent and will change naturally over time.

Now that you've identified your thriver type, it's time to introduce the MOVE framework: the roadmap to closing your fulfillment gap.

CHAPTER 3

MAKE YOUR MOVE: UNDERSTANDING THE FRAMEWORK

Why do accomplished women feel unfulfilled? It's the question at the heart of everything I do—and what I've found is that there are four building blocks underpinning fulfillment: motivation, opportunities, vision, and encouraging community. While each has been studied separately, their integration creates sustainable fulfillment, especially for women navigating systems not designed with us in mind.

Xenia was eloquent, dynamic, and thoughtful—the ideal participant in my four-month group coaching program. What Xenia noticed during our time together was a recurring theme: Her reluctance and fear of professional change had impeded her career aspirations.

She'd been interim deputy director for a nonprofit for almost ten months, leading a team of eight professionals, when a director from another unit was assigned to head the team. Xenia felt sidelined, especially after being asked to resume her managerial role under someone else. She had been enjoying a bit more responsibility. It was giving her the opportunity to experience more exposure, work on more visible projects, and be a part of strategic conversations. Much of this access would now go away, and despite a number of conversations with her supervisor, it didn't appear that this type of opportunity would present itself again any time soon. She saw little hope for a promotion and believed that leaving the organization was the only way forward. But she was also scared of the unknown and wasn't sure what options she would have or even where to start. What guarantee did she have that another role would provide a better-suited career?

Like so many of my clients, Xenia had come to an impasse. She knew she wanted something different—more responsibility, more challenge—but couldn't articulate what that looked like. Xenia needed help gaining a better understanding of herself, her values, and what was driving her toward wanting change. In this chapter, I'll walk you through how I used the MOVE framework with Xenia and how you can use it in your own life.

Once Xenia understood how her hesitation to embrace risk had become a hurdle to her aspirations, we were able to work on identifying opportunities, creating a vision, and tapping into her community ties and network to support the work ahead. But it didn't happen in one fell swoop for Xenia, just like it doesn't happen that way for most of us. Through the MOVE framework you're going to understand the **what**, the **why**, and most importantly the **how** to go about creating the work life you want—just like Xenia and so many others have.

MOVE IN THE MAKING

When professional women successfully recreate their careers, they're *motivated* by a desire for personal fulfillment, whether that's a desire to help others or to seek flexibility. They're able to overcome personal/emotional hurdles such as insecurity and loneliness and find *opportunities* as a result. They identify a *vision* for themselves that guides their goals and they are *encouraged* by their community (be it friends, colleagues, or family).

Now let's dive deeper into each building block:

THE MOVE FRAMEWORK©

M is for Motivation: This is your internal drive. It's what gets you out of bed in the morning, which can be broken down into three parts:

- Values: What truly matters to you? Beyond just paying the bills.
- Skills: What are you fantastic at (even if you don't always give yourself credit)?
- Recognition: Where do you feel valued, and where are you still waiting for that gold star?

> ⁹⁹ *M* is for Motivation: This is your internal drive. It's what gets you out of bed in the morning.

Motivation comes from a deeper well of personal meaning and satisfaction. It's the difference between being pushed by circumstances or drawn by desire. Your unique motivational footprint combines your values, your skills, and recognition.

O is for Opportunities: Doors, windows, hidden trapdoors—let's find them all.

- Access to Networks: Because who you know makes a difference.
- Work Ecosystem: Is your current workplace working for you—or against you?
- Growth Mindset: Embracing challenges and learning from setbacks fuels growth.

> ⁹⁹ *O* is for Opportunities: Doors, windows, hidden trapdoors-let's find them all.

Opportunities are where you can proactively make inroads, be it your network of friends and acquaintances or your colleagues at work. Your ability to create, nurture, and act on these opportunities depends on your internal readiness or mindset.

V is for Vision: What's your North Star?

- Current Self: Who are you today?

- The Active Learning Path: The roadmap guiding you from where you are to where you want to be.
- Future Self: The bold, brilliant version of you that you are becoming.

> ❞ *V* is for Vision: What's your North Star?

Your vision can be viewed as the difference between having a destination and having a compass. Both are useful, but vision points you toward your goals particularly when the terrain shifts unexpectedly. Your vision helps you evaluate opportunities that come your way and set your priorities.

E is for Encouraging Community—Because none of us can do this alone.

Your community is made up of your acquaintances, friends, family, peers—anyone and everyone who you have in your circle and whom you can lean on or learn from at any given time. Your community is your backbone, and they have your back. Consider them your personal cheerleading squad.

> ❞ *E* is for Encouraging Community-
> Because none of us can do this alone.

Unlike frameworks that tell you to find your passion or follow your purpose, MOVE recognizes that fulfillment comes from multiple sources working together. And unlike linear career planning, MOVE is cyclical. You can explore any point and return to any element as you see fit. MOVE recognizes that fulfillment isn't just about finding the perfect job. It's about consciously exploring and developing these four interconnected parts throughout your career and life. Each building block complements the others, creating a foundation for professional joy and personal well-being. When these building blocks work in tandem they bring you work-life integration that fuels continuous growth and deep satisfaction. Now that you understand the MOVE framework, you're ready to dive into how to put each building block into practice.

MOVE IN ACTION

Xenia proudly waved her copious notes and scribbles she had jotted down during our program together. We had covered a variety of topics, ranging from mindset to vision, so when we started working together individually, she had already gained some clarity about her career aspirations.

First, I shared the visual of the MOVE framework that would serve as the backdrop to our coaching journey. I had her rate her level of satisfaction and clarity for all four building blocks (motivation, opportunities, vision, encouraging community) on a scale of 1–10 (10 being the highest).

Xenia rated her motivation as high, a 9/10, and in particular observed that recognition for her skills was of great importance to her. That made sense since being overlooked for a promotion that she believed should have been hers was soul destroying, to say the least. While she received recognition from peers over the years, it was no longer enough. She wanted more for herself. Her motivation was now fueled by a desire for more visibility and responsibility. She felt energized in thinking about continuing in a more senior role. These last ten months as deputy director had given her a taste of what she craved: leadership in action.

Next I posed a question: "What nourishes you?" Her initial reaction was to list all of the team management wins and the recognition she received from peers, but as she exhausted these external motivators, her language started to shift. She realized that a large part of nourishment was also about getting some rest. That was an aha moment! Rest seemed antithetical to the go-go-go mentality she'd believed was the road to success all these years. So, she decided to take a weekend break to do some soul searching. I invited her to pack a list of prompt questions in her weekend bag.

Here are a few:

- What values are you stepping over in staying put in this organization?
- What would a nourished Xenia be wanting for herself? What would be different?
- What skills are you most wanting to use in your next role?
- What do you observe about yourself if you take a helicopter view of your current situation?

Xenia also chose to share this homework with her partner (her encouraging community), and together they talked through some of these questions and added their own reflections. While she didn't make any earth-shattering decisions that restful weekend, she did acknowledge that it gave her space to reconnect with her values and re-energized her to actively search for a more fulfilling role.

After the weekend break, we then turned our attention to the opportunities that she could explore. Rather than default to a mad scramble and job search on LinkedIn, I had her first think through what opportunities were already available to her. I asked her to do an audit of her network: Who did she know? Who did she *need* to know? Who could she already count on for guidance, advice, information, or networking connections?

We also took stock of her current work ecosystem (the environment in which she worked, including the operational aspects such as her team, her role and responsibilities, and the strategic aspects, the company culture, the benefits, and so on) to get clear on what aspects she enjoyed in her present role. Once we identified that, I asked Xenia what she was hoping to find in her next job.

The next time we met, we explored her mindset, looking to unpack the fear behind not daring to apply to positions. She expressed that her current role was, as she put it, "the devil you know." She wasn't prepared to step into discomfort by exploring new opportunities. Again, we worked to help her gain confidence for this next move. The goal was for her to have more clarity on what narrative she could actually control and influence so she could approach her work life through a lens of optimism and opportunity.

Our conversations also gave Xenia the opportunity to revisit her vision. We had already established who she was at that moment (her current self, the one who was sidelined from the role she thought should be hers), and we knew her motivation was to secure a senior role in an organization. The action for her was to close that gap: to find her dream job.

Now she was ready to move into action. Xenia set about activating her network of connections and started applying to roles strategically, taking into account the work that we had covered together. She was deliberate about which positions, within which companies, she would apply to, analyzing their cultures and asking her network for any information she was missing to be able to make an informed decision.

Within five months, she had received several rejections but also two offers, both director positions. One was for a small company with the same title, the other was for a role within a large division with more clout and a renowned brand name. She chose the latter, because she was highly motivated to be recognized as a leader in her field globally. But she was concerned that she could be overworked and acknowledged that she would need to be monitoring her work life regularly so as to avoid burnout. Part of avoiding pressing too hard on the gas at work was the knowledge that she needed to lean on her partner, family, and friends, whom she checked in with regularly over the course of her search. It was important for her to have her cheerleading squad at hand because stepping into the unknown after ten years at her previous company was a hard yet brave decision.

Taking the time to reconnect with who she was and what she wanted gave Xenia the chance to understand her *why* and her *what* so she could choose her next role with confidence and find the fulfillment she had been searching for.

Key Points:

- **Learn the Moves:** Before making any career tweaks or changes, you need clarity on your values, skills, what nourishes you and not just external markers.
- **Your Road Map Is Ready:** The four building blocks of the MOVE framework are your scaffolding for sustainable change.
- **Opportunities Abound:** Audit what's available to you now—your network, your current work ecosystem, and untapped connections that can open doors.
- **Mindset Matters:** Addressing internal barriers like fear of the unknown and discomfort with change is essential to moving forward. What you can control and influence shapes your path.
- **Your Community Is Your Backbone:** Whether it's a partner, family, or friends, having an encouraging support system to lean on is essential for navigating uncertainty and staying focused on your aspirations.

PART II

MOTIVATION: PROPELLING YOU FORWARD

Uncovering what drives you at your core

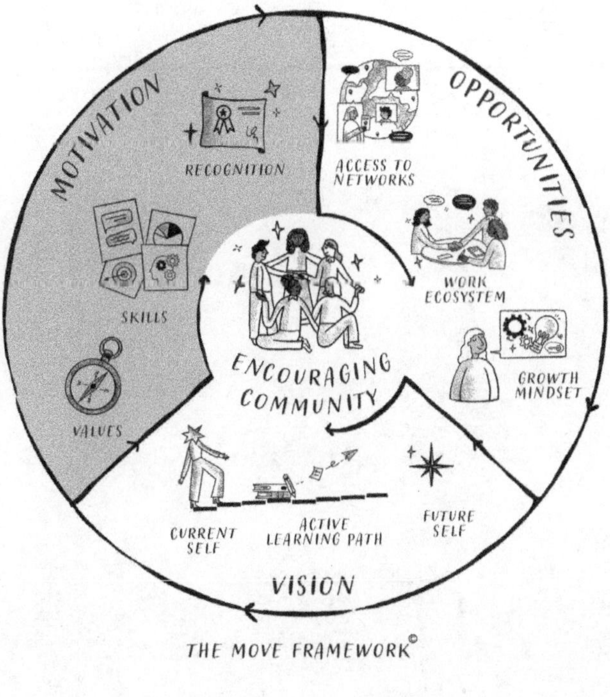

THE MOVE FRAMEWORK©

CHAPTER 4

MOTIVATION: WHAT BRINGS YOU HERE?

Dotted across the globe are women whom I've had the opportunity to speak with, either via Zoom or in person, about the state of their career and their aspirations. Without a doubt, in every conversation, the topic turns to *what: What* brings you to this cohort, workshop, seminar? *What* are you looking to solve during our time together?

Besides a search for connection and community, the main pain point that drives women to these sessions is a discomfort or disillusionment with an aspect of their work life. They show up because there is a new awareness, the tiniest spark that has ignited in them, creating an internal stir, a mini movement. This is why motivation is the first part of the MOVE framework. The spark points us in a new direction, toward *something,* even when the destination remains unknown.

Research shows that when you feel connected to what motivates you, you're more likely to follow through, stay engaged, and feel fulfilled. But how do you know what motivates you? Righting an injustice; seeking better work-life balance; being bored at work, pursuing a long-held dream, or crafting a different lifestyle are all potential motivations.

But the common thread is an inner stirring or pull rather than a push towards external rewards. Think of motivation as both your map and your battery. The map shows you the direction you're going, while the battery supplies the charge. When your battery is low, progress stalls. When you're not following your map, you won't reach your destination. The good news is that you can recharge by reconnecting to what's important to you, which in turn helps you find your way. Motivation is therefore the launch pad for the MOVE framework. Motivation is not just about what you want — it is a reflection of who you are at your essence. At the heart of **Motivation** are values, skills, and recognition, the three elements that, when aligned, create engagement and direction. We begin with **Values** because they guide us toward our aspirations and vision. They are the non-negotiables that make progress feel authentic and turn it into meaningful movement. The truth is that many people struggle with finding fulfillment not because they lack goals, but because they lack sufficient motivation to start and sustain new behavior.

Skills are our capabilities. They are what we *do.* As Malcolm Gladwell, author of *Outliers: The Story of Success,* writes, "Practice isn't the thing you do once you're good. It's the thing you do that makes you good." Gladwell points to the "ten-thousand-hour rule," which states that any skill can be honed with at least ten thousand hours of work, or elbow grease. Even if you're Beyoncé, a naturally gifted singer, you still need to put in the hours to maintain that level of talent. No matter who you are or how you acquire your skills, they are a driver that motivates you.

Now if you think about a positive work experience, what were some of the things you were *doing* that allowed you to knock it out of the park? What skills were you excited to have the chance to use? Knowing which skills are your strong suit will help point you toward a fulfilling work life. But that's not all it takes. There's also **Recognition**, which is how others value your skills and abilities, whether friends, peers, or work colleagues. All of us want to feel recognized for our contributions and rewarded with a simple: "great job" or "thank you." Countless studies on motivation reveal that individuals who are able to use their skill set, act in alignment with their values, and receive recognition for their contributions experience the highest levels of motivation and engagement.

CHAPTER 5

VALUES: EXPLORING YOUR CORE

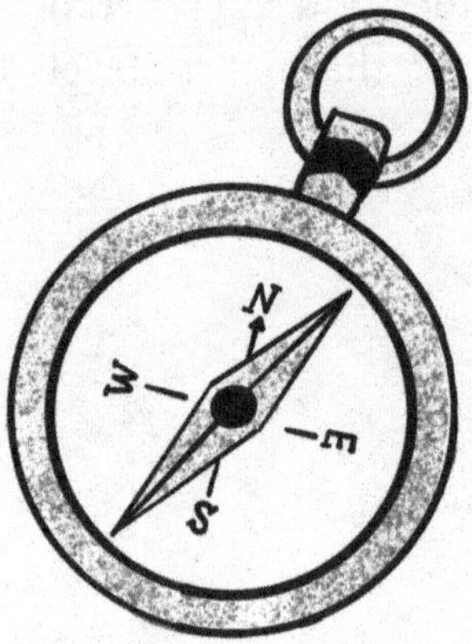

Ask yourself: What matters most to me in my life?

The answer reveals your values. Your values are the needle on your compass, that tiny pointer that helps determine orientation and navigation. Values are shaped by your identity, priorities, and goals. They are influenced by your personal relationships and by society. They guide how you express yourself in the world and what you are drawn to exploring and doing with your life.

Values are data. Your trusted travel companions. They shape your life path and impact the choices you make at any given moment. For example, if you value service, you might choose to prioritize volunteering experiences over material possessions. If you value time, you might choose a career that allows for more flexibility and remote work.

”Values are data.

Values are particularly helpful when faced with difficult choices, as is often the case in career exploration. Values help you figure out what brings you joy when life feels murky and unclear. Over the course of your work life, you will likely encounter moments of misalignment with your values. As my good friend Sarah Young, CEO of Zing Collaborative, wrote in her book *Expansive Impact*, “Everyday choices and actions are micro-level votes for either the type of person you want to be or the type of person you don’t want to be. Honoring our values through our actions is casting a vote for our highest self.”

ZARA’S STORY

Zara, whom you met in the introduction, was someone who aligned her actions with her values. In one of our sessions she was reviewing Brené Brown’s downloadable list of more than one hundred values. We skimmed the list, over and over: everything from adaptability, courage, and freedom to resourcefulness, tradition, and responsibility, and I encouraged her to add any of her own that were missing. I wanted her to spend time thinking about each of these values. Then came the crucial step: choosing her top ten values from the list of one hundred and then eventually narrowing it down to her top five. I encouraged Zara to move quickly as she did the exercise so she wouldn't overanalyze too much. After twenty minutes, Zara revealed the five values that were most important to her: flexibility, recognition, service, excellence, and relationships.

Once Zara had homed in on her top values, we dove into reflective prompts to better understand how she functions. When do these values show up most powerfully? When did she feel misaligned with them? What's happening in those moments? These questions helped Zara uncover any friction points and gain insights on how to align her actions with what she was seeking for herself.

To pressure-test her values, I asked Zara to go home and try what I've done in group sessions: Find someone to pair up with and give them permission to narrow down her list of five values to three. I explained that her reaction to having her value erased was a sure-fire way of knowing whether it was truly important to her. For example, if you've listed financial security, autonomy, kindness, inclusion, and service and someone crosses out service, which is fundamental to you, you'll most likely have a visceral reaction. I've watched people during this activity let out audible gasps when they had a value removed that was critical to them.

Listen to your body. It will lead the way.

Listen to your body. It will lead the way.

VALUES AS A CATALYST

This same activity was a thunderbolt for Nora, a brand manager who joined a career networking event I was co-leading at Unilever in London. As part of the workshop, attendees paired up and exchanged insights based on prompts such as: What could you not live without doing? At the end of your life, if you hadn't done it, what would be a powerful regret? What would you do if you knew you wouldn't fail?

Something happened for Nora that evening as she shared her story. She revealed that she had experienced a traumatic birth, and she could not let go of her realization that, because of her social status, she had been able to get the help and access to the support she needed. But she recalled that this was not the case for many women, particularly women of color. As she was reviewing her responses to the prompts and sharing her insights with her group, she told me it hit her there and then: If she didn't address this situation, she wouldn't be able to live with herself going forward. The conversations that evening led her to start a side business supporting Black women in having positive birthing experiences. It was as though a dam had opened, and she felt propelled to launch something that would change lives for the better.

Nora didn't upend her life but rather rearranged it to fit in something that was valuable to her. She stayed at her job, which provided the financial safety net she needed, and launched her side business too. She worked on it in the evenings and on weekends. Being able to align with her values while not rocking the boat of her family responsibilities brought her joy and contentment. She did have to forfeit some weekend activities, but she knew it was temporary. Defining your values is about getting ready to explore your "what's next?" You can't begin the exploratory process without getting clear on what you value, as this will help you make informed choices.

VALUES IN ACTION

Think about someone you deeply respect: maybe a colleague, mentor, or public figure. What is it about them that you admire? Usually it's not only their achievements, but how they show up. That's their values in action.

Maybe they're someone who speaks up for others when it's uncomfortable. Maybe they're someone who maintains boundaries even when it's hard to do so. Maybe they're someone who always shows up to help a friend in need. These behavioral patterns reveal their core values.

Sometimes it's hard for people to think about what they value, but have a look at what they spend their time and money on (their values in action), and that's a clear indicator. Are you an online shopper? Are you always volunteering to help out at school? Whatever you find yourself doing often enough is insight into what you value. I know I find myself scrolling through online classes because I value learning.

What do you value? Does where you spend your time align with what you say you value? What patterns are starting to emerge as you think about where your time and attention naturally flow?

ACTIVITY: SURFACING YOUR VALUES: WHAT MATTERS TO YOU MOST

Values clarification is a foundational practice in career coaching and positive psychology. This exercise will help you identify which values matter most to you and how to bring them to life through action.

Part I: Identify Your Core Values

Review the list of values and notice which ones resonate with you. Circle ten to fifteen values that feel most important to you right now. Don't overthink this; go with your gut. If you're torn between two similar values, choose both for now. Feel free to add any values that are important to you but missing from the list.

Common Values:

Accomplishment • Accuracy • Adventure • Affection • Authenticity • Authority • Autonomy • Balance • Beauty • Belonging • Caring • Challenge • Change • Collaboration • Commitment • Community • Compassion • Competence • Connection • Contribution • Courage • Creativity • Curiosity • Dependability • Determination • Discovery • Empathy • Enjoyment • Excellence • Excitement • Fairness • Faith • Family • Financial stability • Fitness • Flexibility • Freedom • Friendship • Fun • Generosity • Genuineness • Growth • Harmony • Health • Honesty • Hope • Humility • Humor • Impact • Independence • Influence •

Inner peace • Innovation • Integrity • Justice • Kindness • Knowledge • Leadership • Learning • Legacy • Leisure • Love • Loyalty • Making a difference • Mastery • Meaning • Mindfulness • Nature • Openness • Order • Passion • Patience • Peace • Perseverance • Personal development • Play • Pleasure • Power • Purpose • Quality • Recognition • Relationships • Reliability • Respect • Responsibility • Risk-taking • Romance • Safety • Security • Self-discipline • Self-expression • Serenity • Service • Simplicity • Solitude • Spirituality • Spontaneity • Stability • Status • Stewardship • Strength • Success • Sustainability • Teamwork • Thoughtfulness • Tradition • Tranquility • Travel • Trust • Truth • Understanding • Uniqueness • Variety • Vitality • Vulnerability • Wealth • Well-being • Wholeheartedness • Wisdom • Wonder • Work-life integration

Add your own:

Part II: Narrow to Your Top Five

Review your list of ten to fifteen and ask yourself: If I could only honor five of these values in my life and work, which would they be? This is the hard part. Cross out the others and write your top five here:

1 ________________________________

2 ________________________________

3 ________________________________

4 ________________________________

5 ________________________________

Part III: How Your Values Come Alive

Values become meaningful when we translate them into action. As Sarah Young reminds us, everyday choices are micro-level votes for the type of person we want to be. In this next step, you'll identify how each of your values shows up in both your work and personal life. For each value, write specific activities or behaviors that bring this value to life. Think about both professional and personal contexts. Ask yourself: What am I doing when this value is most alive in me? How does this value guide my choices at work and beyond?

For example, here's how my values show up across work and life:

LEARNING	ENROLLING IN EXECUTIVE EDUCATION COURSES, ATTENDING INDUSTRY CONFERENCES AND READING RESEARCH ON THE FUTURE OF WORK
SERVICE	FACILITATING LEADERSHIP WORKSHOPS, COACHING CLIENTS, OFFERING PRO-BONO CONSULTING TO NON-PROFIT ORGANIZATIONS
CREATIVITY	DESIGNING EXPERIENTIAL WORKSHOPS AND CREATING NEW COACHING TOOLS AND WRITTEN CONTENT
CONNECTION	MAKING TIME FOR REGULAR MEETUPS WITH FRIENDS AND MAINTAINING CLOSE RELATIONSHIPS ACROSS MULTIPLE TIME ZONES
JOY	PLANNING REGULAR TRIPS AND PRIORITIZING SHARED EXPERIENCES WITH FRIENDS

Notice how each value is expressed through repeatable behaviors, not just intentions.

Now it's your turn:

YOUR TURN

Part IV: Reality Check

Looking at your five values and their actions, estimate what percentage of your week currently goes toward each:

REALITY CHECK

1 ______________________ %

2 ______________________ %

3 ______________________ %

4 ______________________ %

5 ______________________ %

Which value is getting the most time? Which is getting the least? Where's the gap between what you say matters and where your time actually goes?

Notice which values feel most alive and which feel dormant.

Now reflect on the following questions:

- Where do your values get the most expression in your current life?
- Which values need more time/space in your life?
- What activities could you reduce to make room for value-aligned activities?
- How might you bring one of these values to life this week?

Practical Steps:

Start this week by choosing one value that needs more expression. Identify a fifteen-minute action you can take to honor it and put it in your calendar. Going forward, check in with yourself by asking: Have my actions this week been aligned with my values? If not, how can I bring how I spend my time closer to my values? For example, if one of your core values is creativity, a goal might be to spend thirty minutes each day on an art project.

Values work doesn't have to be a solo voyage. In fact, it's often more insightful when someone else can hold up a mirror for us. Think of a person in your life who sees you in action on a regular basis and cares about your growth. You could share your top three to five values with that person and ask them to check in with you via text once a week with two simple questions: Which of your values got the most expression this week? Which were muted?

This work requires ongoing reflection and adjustment. What I've learned through this process is that small value shifts can lead to profound changes in your level of energy and fulfillment.

In our next chapter, we'll explore how your skills intersect with your values. Discovering how your unique abilities and skill sets can bring your values to life will help you get one step closer to fulfillment.

Key Points:

- **Define Your Values:** Understand what your core values are and how they provide direction in your life so they become your own personal compass for decision-making.
- **Identify Value Gaps:** Recognize which values are most important and which have been neglected given your current lifestyle and work. Do a time audit to pinpoint which of your stated values are aligned with how you spend your time and which aren't.
- **Enhance Your Self-Awareness:** Recognize how your values contribute to your sense of who you are and what you're seeking in your work and life.

CHAPTER 6

SKILLS: HARNESSING YOUR STRENGTHS

Charlotte, a seasoned lawyer, realized after nine years at her company that she didn't really have anywhere else to grow in-house. She was ready to move out of corporate, but she had always been a lawyer and couldn't imagine what else she could do. "It took me some time to be able to identify my skills and learn ways to reassure the start-ups I wanted to work with that I wasn't *just* a lawyer," she told me when I interviewed her for my research.

Charlotte's story reflects a challenge many women face. When you've been in one role for a long time, it becomes easy to see yourself only through the narrow lens of the skills you've been using forever. Yes, Charlotte was a successful tax lawyer, but she could no longer see past her job title to recognize the transferable skills that made her valuable beyond the legal field. She was stuck. Despite being highly qualified, she felt inadequate and unprepared to explore other options with confidence. She just didn't know how to pitch herself.

Research from Siri Terjesen, founding executive director of the Madden Center for Value Creation at Florida Atlantic University, shows that women who intentionally tapped into their strengths gained greater flexibility in creating and choosing new work opportunities. But how do you know what your skill sets are?

The truth is that skill sets aren't something we're born with. They're developed through practice, lots and lots of practice. True expertise in any skill is about doing the same thing over and over until it becomes second nature. And once we become an expert, our self-esteem and confidence in that area increases too, which has the domino effect of creating more self-assurance, hence more comfort with what we know how to do. Feeling confident motivates us to keep perfecting our skill set. Yet taking those same skills and transposing them to another type of job may prove daunting because you can't know for certain that those skills will work in another setting. The key here is to focus on the skills that you are drawn to, the skills that give you energy, and then try them in different scenarios.

Groundbreaking books like *What Color Is Your Parachute?* and *Who Moved My Cheese?* were revolutionary because they brought to the forefront that your skill set is your strength and focusing on what you're good at will lead you to a role that's a good match. The reason these books resonated so deeply is that they reminded us that our skills are our differentiators, but only when you know which ones bring you into the flow zone.

> **Our skills are our differentiators, but only when you know which ones bring you into the flow zone.**

YOUR SKILL SET IS YOUR THRILL SET

What Charlotte discovered and what many women looking to make a change, whether big or small, have found is that identifying their skills is one piece of the puzzle. Being able to connect or reconnect with those skills that energize you is where the thrill comes in.

When you use the skills you're good at in your daily work, you will automatically feel more engaged. Research in positive psychology shows that applying your signature strengths at work is linked to higher engagement and satisfaction. The more you lean into skills you've honed, the more confident and motivated you feel, which in turn increases your self-confidence to tackle challenges. Skills that give you a thrill point you toward opportunities where you will thrive.

This is the difference between simply cataloging the tasks you do and uncovering what makes you come alive. So how can you identify your skill set and leverage it to drive your motivation?

CASE STUDY: SHANI'S STORY

Shani, an HR business partner at a small advertising agency, was invited to speak on a few panels on The Future of Work. She had been with the same company for four years and chose to invest in coaching sessions because she was looking for help in finding more fulfillment at work. We started off by looking to see what she might want to tweak about her current situation. She admitted that she enjoyed her job but was feeling unmotivated and in need of some direction in order to stay engaged. "Do you know what it is?" Shani said. "I'm embarrassed to say it, but I'm often bored at work." She paused and looked at me with a smile on her face. "I really want a passion project, something that takes me out of my regular work. I want to have more variety in my current role, and I don't know how to ask for that."

Public speaking was something Shani was interested in becoming more actively involved in. She had recently had the chance to speak at the town hall in front of her whole company and she wanted to try something that tapped into more than her people and project-management skills. "The feedback was so good. My director said I was a confident and engaging speaker who used clear, well-structured storytelling to share HR updates and data. Colleagues mentioned how comfortable I seemed and how I weaved different stories with humor to create an insightful conversation."

This was the perfect introduction to delve into the skills she utilized in that town hall meeting to understand her abilities outside her day-to-day role. She was positively beaming when she recounted what her colleagues had told her. In being recognized for her strengths, Shani could see a path toward infusing more joy in her work life.

One exercise (a crowd-pleaser, as I like to say) is called MIME, "My Incredible Momentous Experience," which is based on an activity I was first introduced to during my certification as a career counselling coach. In this activity, you reflect on two moments in your work life where you have felt an immense sense of accomplishment and satisfaction, where you were fully in the flow of your work. Next you take a large sheet of paper and turn it horizontally. On the top of the sheet, you write out the two examples, in capital letters for good measure, and then create two columns. On the left-hand side, just as below, you write down the skills that you use for each example, and on the right-hand side, you write down the environment that supported your examples and that made it such a positive experience.

I asked Shani to do the MIME exercise. On the left-hand side, I had her list all the skills she felt she was using in that moment, and on the right-hand side I had her list the conditions which enabled these skills to shine. Then I asked her for a second work example, but she couldn't think of one. She seemed troubled by that, but I explained that the aim was for her to uncover her strengths in life *and* work, so I invited her to pick an example from her life. Shani spoke about organizing her sister's wedding, which she had done the prior year. She was the wedding planner and loved every minute of it. When I probed her to tell me what gave her so much joy in that mammoth project, she said giving the maid of honor speech was the highlight. Not a dry eye in the room!

We explored the skills she had used and the conditions that made this such an optimal experience (here's what she wrote):

ORGANIZING MY SISTER'S WEDDING

SKILLS	ENVIRONMENT
✦ PUBLIC SPEAKING (TO A LARGE AUDIENCE)	✦ CLOSE FAMILY AND FRIENDS
✦ STORYTELLING	✦ DIVERSE GROUP OF PEOPLE
✦ PROJECT COORDINATION	✦ A SUPPORTIVE ENVIRONMENT
✦ RELATIONSHIP MANAGEMENT AND DIPLOMACY	✦ A STUNNING VENUE
✦ CREATING CONNECTION AND SAFETY	✦ PROFESSIONAL LOGISTICS, IT, MUSIC ETC.THAT MADE FOR A HICCUP-FREE EVENING

We then looked at the skills and conditions that overlapped in both examples that she had given: public speaking, building psychological safety, storytelling, and creating connections within groups of people. The conditions in both scenarios showed how much she valued diverse groups of people, how comfortable she was being behind the scenes and on stage, and, most importantly, how much she thrived being in situations that involved helping others in creating a positive impact.

Shani realized in looking at the experience of speaking at the town hall and helping plan her sister's wedding that she came alive when she was able to combine her organizational skills with opportunities to connect with people through storytelling. This helped her to see how important speaking opportunities were for her and how that would bring her more joy. Going forward, she prioritized expanding her HR network by volunteering to sit on panels and speak at events. She looked for moments that made her feel in connection with others. She joined an employee resource group focused on internal communication, which gave her the chance to volunteer for speaking opportunities and help craft messages that connected with employees. She was soon more energized and engaged than before without having had to seek out external opportunities.

FINDING YOUR SKILLS SWEET SPOT

Have you ever noticed that if you reflect on key moments when you're feeling your best, and utilizing skills that you enjoy, you enter what psychologists Mihaly Csikszentmihalyi and Jeanne Nakamura call a flow state, a period of time when conditions are optimal and you find yourself coasting with ease? This is the result of having both your skills and the conditions in which you find yourself in complete sync.

Understanding the moments you feel in flow is essential, but there's something else to consider. Not every skill that you enjoy will align with your career aspirations, and not every skill you possess brings you joy. This is where finding your *skills sweet spot* becomes essential. To explore this intersection, I invite you to try the **skill sweet spot activity** below. This isn't about conducting a skills audit or finding what you're lacking. Instead, you're going on a scavenger hunt to uncover talents you may have forgotten you had.

This activity works best in two parts because sometimes the best insights come to the surface after a good night's sleep. As always, be sure to set some time aside and to take notes, whether on your computer, your phone, or with pen and paper.

ACTIVITY: SKILL SWEET SPOT

You're going to start by writing down all your skills off the top of your head. Some prompts to use as thought starters:

- What do people naturally turn to you for?
- What comes easily for you but is harder for others?
- What tasks do you find yourself returning to even though they are difficult?

Once you have at least twelve skills jotted down, sort them into four buckets:

Skills That Thrill: Time disappears when you're using these skills.

Skills You're Good at but Make You Pout: You're competent in these areas, but they don't spark joy.

Skills That Excite Your Future Self: These are ones you're looking to develop for Future You.

Skills Others High-Five You About: The things people consistently appreciate and compliment you on.

Let your list sit for twenty-four hours. Then review your list with fresh eyes. Are there any skills that no longer fit in a particular category?

Now highlight the skills that appear in "Skills That Thrill" and "Skills Others High-Five You About." These are your signature strengths. Reflect on these skills. How much does your current work environment provide the conditions for your skills to shine? How can you create more opportunities that bring out your strengths, be it volunteering, building a side project, or even a hobby?

ELENA'S STORY:

Elena, a program coordinator at the United Nations, had spent many years in international relations managing stakeholder relationships. When given the opportunity, she jumped at the chance to join a coaching program for women working at the UN that I was running. She had been working in one of the smaller offices in Ethiopia for a few years and was feeling isolated, overworked, and demotivated. Even though working in the field had been her dream, five years in, she was ready to explore other options. In the coaching program we worked on reflective activities that help with skills exploration, values, and vision. A month after the program ended, Elena shared that she had revisited the skills sweet spot exercise and she was surprised by what emerged as she jotted down her answers:

Skills That Thrill: One-on-one conversations where she helped people work through challenges, creating calm in chaotic situations, explaining the intricacies of stakeholder management, listening deeply, helping people feel heard and acknowledged.

Skills I'm Good at but Make Me Pout: Writing briefs, meeting scheduling, maintaining databases, heavy bureaucracy.

Skills That Excite My Future Self: Holistic health practices, helping people with stress management, creating supportive spaces, working more independently.

Skills Others High-Five Me About: She was often told that she had a calming presence, that she was a great listener. A number of colleagues had even commented on how she'd introduced them to breathing techniques and mindfulness practices that helped them manage work stress.

After putting her answers to one side for a few days, Elena saw the overlap clearly: the one-on-one support, creating a calming environment, helping people feel heard and grounded; these showed up in both columns.

She noticed that while she was good at coordination work, what energized her most was supporting people's well-being. She had always followed wellness videos and had gone on a few retreats for that very purpose over her holidays. She was really intrigued with doing a deeper dive into this space. She decided to leave the United Nations and embark on a wellness course, to become a yoga and wellness instructor, the path toward becoming a health and wellness coach. She was building a career around the skills that brought her fulfillment. Today she works with teams helping them build wellness practices. She uses her coordination skills in service of work that thrills her.

WHY RELATIONAL SKILLS MATTER

I've found that the skill set that is most often overlooked is relational skills, and that's because, let's face it, those are the skills that women tend to be best at. Women are generally more relationally oriented than men. It comes naturally to many of us and shouldn't be underestimated. Listening, seeking harmony, caretaking, and creating psychological safety are not nice-to-haves, but must-haves in most areas of life.

In a seminal research study titled *Women's Ways of Knowing,* Mary Field Belenky, Blythe McVicker Clinchy, Nancy Rule Goldberger, and Jill Mattuck Tarule talk about something they call connected knowing, which emphasizes empathy, perspective-taking, listening, and learning through relationship. These are often viewed as soft skills not worthy of true leaders. But Gallup research suggests that interpersonal skills aren't just "soft" skills but fundamental drivers of career fulfillment and organizational success. What we might dismiss as "just being nice" could actually be our greatest professional asset.

This brings us back to Charlotte's dilemma. Charlotte, as you might remember, had nowhere to grow in-house, so when we started working together, we focused on making sure she had a solid idea of her strengths. In one of our sessions, I asked her to make two lists. On one side, she listed her job responsibilities—contract negotiation, regulatory compliance, tax planning, risk assessment. On the other side, she highlighted the aspects of her job that she loved to do. She was drawn to analyzing complex business scenarios under tight deadlines, translating dense legal concepts into clear strategic guidance, and thriving in high-pressure situations where decisions had significant consequences. She loved the variety of issues that crossed her desk and the quick turnarounds that kept her sharp. These skills were her energy givers. Those skills—distilling complexity, making critical decisions quickly, staying sharp when stakes are high, and pivoting between different challenges—were exactly what startups needed. She just needed to learn how to articulate them in her resume and when she went on job interviews.

I often hear people say: "Am I enough, do I know enough, do I have sufficient knowledge, the right skills?" We place a lot of weight on our skills, relational and technical, as that is what we're hired for. But we wouldn't last very long in our careers if we didn't also have strong relational skills to help smooth out the inevitable bumps. It's no surprise that when we're seeking any type of career change that we would want reassurance about our skill set to help us stay motivated. Charlotte certainly felt that way.

But it's not just your existing skills that matter. It's the skills you need to acquire that make a difference too. Edina, the former partner in a law firm who launched an NGO, shared that she had a limited understanding of the functioning of a nonprofit when she was starting out. "I didn't know anything about NGOs or nonprofits, I didn't understand basic definitions...." So she began reaching out to people she knew who were in positions that she aspired to reach and started connecting with them. She took people out for coffee and asked questions. She did research. She fast-tracked her skill building without needing to get another degree. The good news is that many of Edina and Charlotte's existing skills provided a stronger foundation for the work they were trying to do than they initially realized. Edina later reflected on how her thirteen years of law practice had actually prepared her well: "When I think back to what helped me, I think certainly the fact that I built confidence with public speaking, with managerial skills, with negotiation, with drafting documents, writing bills, and sitting down with people, convincing them that *X* is the right way to go when they walked in believing *Z* was the correct way."

In the constantly evolving work landscape, keeping your skill set relevant while also ensuring that you understand your strengths so you can take them with you as your career evolves is key. The transformation that is possible when you shift from thinking about job titles to thinking about skills is profound. But let's be clear: You can't always control the conditions in which you find yourself, but you can learn to create conditions that complement the skills you've honed and leverage them intentionally.

Having had a chance to explore the role of skills and values, we will next turn to exploring recognition, the external validation that fuels your motivation and confirms that your contributions matter.

Key Points:

- **Your Skill Set Is Your Thrill Set:** The skills that energize you are your greatest assets. When you use your strengths, you naturally perform better and feel more confident, creating an upward spiral of joy.
- **Flow Moments Reveal Your Blueprint:** Those peak experiences when you were at your best show you the skills and conditions where you naturally excel.
- **Your Signature Strengths Are Hiding in Plain Sight:** The intersection of what you love doing and what

others consistently recognize in you reveals your strengths.

- **Relational Skills Are Real Skills:** Your ability to listen, build trust, create harmony, and make others feel valued aren't soft skills. They're fundamental drivers of career success that women often undervalue.
- **You Are Already Whole:** You don't need to become someone new. You need to recognize and articulate the skills you already have.
- **Small Opportunities Create Big Momentum:** Insights build momentum, one new discovery at a time, and help to close your fulfillment gap.

CHAPTER 7

RECOGNITION: ACKNOWLEDGING YOUR VALUE

I once watched a panel with Oprah at the Tribeca TV Festival where she said that everyone she ever interviewed, including Beyoncé, asked "how did I do?" once the cameras were turned off. Oprah had recorded 4,589 shows and interviewed over 37,000 people by this point, and this question was the "common denominator" for all her guests.

Oprah's reaction to Beyoncé's question after her interview: "Girrrrrrl, you're Beyoncé!" She was clearly surprised that the chart-topping superstar needed the same validation as the rest of us puny humans.

I wasn't shocked though. A Gallup report from 2024 showed that only 22 percent of employees feel their efforts receive enough recognition. Being acknowledged for the work we put in fuels us. Without it, we lose momentum. Yet recognition is a human craving that's sadly often overlooked.

LITTLE SHOP OF HOORAYS

Think of recognition as the clapping that fills a room after a song; it's the encore you hear at the opera, the resounding roar when a goal is scored. It's the energetic and instant response to what you do.

Recognition comes in many forms. It can be everyday praise like a heartfelt thank you, an award, or even a performance review. It can be private—like a conversation with your manager—or a public acknowledgement. No matter what form it takes, recognition is about your work being validated and confirms your contributions matter.

Psychiatrist Anna Fels writes in *Necessary Dreams* that women need two things to feel fulfilled: mastery and recognition. Mastery is when we become so good at what we do that doing the thing becomes a reward in itself. We feel delighted by the skill. But if we don't have a supportive audience that encourages and recognizes us then our skills won't continue to develop over time.

Recognition is about external validation. Without recognition, even the most competent person can feel invisible. And when you feel invisible, motivation withers. It's hard to maintain motivation when others are unaware or unappreciative of your work.

Let me share Julie's story.

Julie sat across from me at 11th Street Cafe, my favorite breakfast haunt in the West Village in New York City, wiping away tears as she tried to compose herself. This wasn't the first time we'd had a conversation, but this time felt different, more desperate. She was visibly emotional, choking back tears. Her lip was quivering, and she was gripping her tea as she shifted in her seat. The reason she was so devastated: For the second time in four months her boss had excluded her from travelling to the events she'd been planning for her team. Julie worked for a French company based in New York specializing in international fashion brand launches, and her job was to ensure the coordination of events. As a trilingual speaker, she should have had the opportunity to travel globally to help on the ground. In fact, her language skills and cultural fluency were the very reasons she was hired, as she could navigate English-, French-, and Spanish-speaking markets seamlessly.

Julie had been working diligently on the team's big event for months, but when *go time* came, she was instructed to stay behind. No explanation was given and certainly no acknowledgment of the work hours and weekends she had put into prepping for the team's success. Julie was crushed. "I just want to quit," she told me, but with no viable options on the table, and the fact that her work visa was tied to her job, leaving was not a realistic option. She felt helpless and hopeless and angry. "I don't even know what I did wrong. I work weekends, I stay late, I respond to emails at midnight. There is no acknowledgement. I am basically invisible."

We started by simply unpacking her emotions. The cafe was empty as it was past the morning rush. As we spoke the coffee machine was gurgling in the background and the barista was rearranging a tray of blueberry muffins behind the counter. "Oftentimes, before you can solve a problem," I told Julie, "you need to acknowledge and validate how you're feeling." Julie nodded. She understood.

"The lack of recognition for my work has diminished my sense of worth," she said, and I reached my hand out toward her across the table. I understood that this was not a headspace from which to brainstorm or explore other work options. She needed a way to reconnect with her own worth.

To give her a boost, I suggested she create a Little Shop of Hoorays folder, a place where she would collect all of the recognition she had received over time, either in person or online, whether from a client, a friend or a peer. At first, she looked skeptical. "What's the point?" she asked. "I don't see how amassing a bunch of old compliments is going to be of help."

I nodded, understanding why she felt that the exercise was hopeless. "But trust me," I said. "Can you do that?" She agreed, wiping away her tears.

Over the following weeks, Julie populated her folder with client thank-you emails, screenshots of Slack messages where colleagues praised her creative skills, photos from past events she'd coordinated seamlessly. Her Little Shop of Hoorays was expanding. It didn't happen overnight, but as she gathered more evidence of her hard work and expertise, her mindset began to shift ever so slightly. The point of the folder is to create a joy repository. The exercise was about reconnecting Julie to her worth, when external validation had dried up. It was about taking stock of all her past accomplishments to rewire her brain to remember, and to shape a narrative that didn't solely depend on one person's acknowledgement—or lack of, in Julie's case.

The goal for Julie was to first reconnect with those moments of encouragement that had given her a boost over the course of her career. She committed to visiting her folder every week. Her mood improved, she found herself in awe of some of what she had been told way back when that she had forgotten about.

Over the next three months, Julie, who had been checking in on her Little Shop weekly, found that something shifted. She had evidence, real evidence, of her abilities and impact. Once Julie regained some of her confidence, we started having conversations about stretch assignments, such as working in another division on a higher-level project. She started having informal conversations with other departments, and while she didn't find a new role, she focused on what she could control and found more fulfillment in her work. Julie's story illustrates what happens when recognition vanishes and your sense of belonging takes a hit. The most important thing to do when that happens is to build your recognition reserve so that it can sustain you through tougher moments.

IT'S ALL IN THE PRAISE

A 2023 Gallup study on recognition revealed that organizations can increase productivity by 9 percent by doubling the number of employees who receive recognition in a given week. For a ten-thousand-employee organization, this means over $90 million in productivity gains alone!

This represents a productivity opportunity that more organizations could benefit from if recognition was embedded more systematically into their workplace culture. Recognition doesn't need to be monetary. In fact, research shows that it's more important that employees feel that their efforts are valued. When you don't you end up, like Julie, feeling invisible.

For women of color, this feeling of invisibility is often more pronounced. Black women have less access to training, receive fewer mentorship and sponsorship opportunities, and have fewer occasions to be in conversation with senior leaders. It becomes a vicious circle. When you're not seen, you can't advance, and when you can't advance, you remain unseen and unrecognized.

> **” Black women have less access to training, receive fewer mentorship and sponsorship opportunities, and have fewer occasions to be in conversation with senior leaders.**

One movie that has stuck with me all these years and points to the phenomenon of invisibility for Black women is *Hidden Figures,* which tells the story of Katherine Johnson, Mary Jackson, Dorothy Vaughan, and Christine Darden, talented Black mathematicians whose calculations were critical to NASA's success, though they weren't recognized for their contributions until decades later. These women were paid less, received fewer opportunities for advancement, and suffered the consequences of segregation, often having to submit their work anonymously to get noticed at all. It wasn't until 2024 (yes, you read that right!) that they were finally awarded with Congressional Gold Medals to spotlight their hard work, including being the brains behind John Glenn's launch into orbit. Not only were these four women's lives and careers hurt by their dismissal, but what stands out to me is the fact that so many younger women missed out on being inspired by these role models. There's no question that decades of invisibility came at a cost. And, unfortunately, this doesn't only happen at NASA but in companies across the globe. Close your eyes for a minute and ask yourself: How many astronauts, mathematicians, and engineers have we lost because women couldn't see themselves in any of these roles? Which is why I always tell my clients not to wait on others to recognize them. Start to build your own recognition practices today.

RECOGNIZING OTHERS

One more element that's critical is the importance of recognizing others. Just as you seek external validation, you're also in a position to shine a light on people in your orbit. You can do that by including a recognition practice weekly or monthly: reflecting on what type of recognition might be most meaningful to the person receiving your praise, and what specifically you would want to acknowledge. This matters because when you become someone who consistently notices and acknowledges others' contributions several delightful things start to happen:

- First, you sharpen your observation skills, which makes you better at recognizing your own contributions too.
- Second, you model the behavior you want to receive. People learn what kind of recognition is valuable by watching what you give.
- Third, you create reciprocity, of the good kind. Spaces where recognition flows freely tend to be places where everyone feels more seen.
- Fourth, giving recognition strengthens relationships. When you take the time to notice what someone else does well and articulate it, you're showing them you see them. That builds trust and connection.

Recognition is your antidote, the thing you can return to when doubt creeps in, when your boss overlooks you, when the credit goes to someone else. Your Little Shop of Hoorays isn't just a folder; it's proof of all the good you do.

When recognition is authentic, it's the ignition you need. You now have the tools to capture, analyze, and give recognition. You understand why it matters and how to create your own repository of worth when external validation runs dry. Recognition requires input from others, which is precisely why we need to design our recognition experiences.

As I mentioned at the start, even Beyoncé asked, "How'd I do?" You're not alone in needing recognition. The difference is whether you're waiting for it or actively building a practice around it.

Now it's your turn to create your own Little Shop of Hoorays that you can access whenever doubt creeps in or external validation runs dry.

ACTIVITY: LITTLE SHOP OF HOORAYS

Start by creating a folder on your computer and give it a name that makes you smile. Some of my clients have called theirs "The Fab File," "Evidence of Awesome," or simply "My Victory Vault." This is a folder of *you* for *you*. Building your self-worth is essential and quite frankly mandatory because unless you have the memory of an elephant, you need a place to capture all praise as soon as it's received. In terms of what to include, think about the following:

- **Email Thank-Yous from Colleagues or Clients:** Screenshot or save emails where someone specifically acknowledges your contribution. Not just "thanks!" but messages that detail what you did and why it mattered.

- **Positive Performance Reviews:** Copy the sentences that highlight your strengths and accomplishments, not just the overall rating.
- **LinkedIn Recommendations and Endorsements:** Screenshot comments or recommendations that speak to your specific skills or character.
- **Slack/Teams Messages:** Capture moments where colleagues publicly praise your work, ask for your expertise, or credit your ideas.
- **Project-Completion Photos or Screenshots:** Visual evidence of work you're proud of: a successful event, a completed presentation, a project launch.
- **Client Testimonials:** Any feedback from customers or stakeholders that show how your work made a difference.
- **Awards or Certificates:** Formal recognition, even if it feels small (employee of the month, training completion, conference presenter badge). I have all of my conference badges hanging up—not in my folder but behind my office door where I can see them regularly.
- **Your Own Notes and Scribbles:** Write down any verbal compliments you've received.

Now comes the essential part, set a reminder to spend five to ten minutes adding to your Shop every week. Ask yourself:

- What went well this week?
- What feedback did I receive?
- What am I proud of, even if no one else noticed?

Stefanie Sword-Williams, author of *F*ck Being Humble* and *Career Comedown: What to Do When Work Isn't Working for You,* outlines an activity she started during lockdown where every Friday before dinner she and a friend would reflect on two to three things they had done that week that they were happy about and then voice note these wins to practice verbalizing their success. They called it "wins before dins." The power of this practice isn't just in creating a folder and hoarding positive statements, it's in maintaining the habit of adding to it. Weekly additions train your mind to notice and value your own contributions, which gradually shifts how you view yourself. This daily practice of noticing is essential. And there is another layer to build a robust recognition practice: understanding where your recognition comes from.

ACTIVITY: SORT YOUR SOURCES OF RECOGNITION

Now that you've created your Little Shop of Hoorays, take it a step further. This activity helps you understand where your recognition is coming from so you can identify any gaps or patterns. Go through your Little Shop of Hoorays and sort your acknowledgments by source. You might write them on sticky notes grouped by category, or simply note the source next to each item:

- Work
- Personal

- Community
- Self

Then reflect:

- Which areas are most abundant? Which are less so?
- How recognized do you feel across these different areas of your life?
- What patterns are you noticing?

The goal isn't perfect balance across all categories but rather to understand where your recognition comes from and where you might need more to stay energized and motivated.

WHY THIS MATTERS

Diversifying your sources of recognition is important so as not to have an overreliance (as was the case with Julie) on one source.

- If all your recognition comes from work, what happens when you have a challenging boss? Your sense of worth becomes vulnerable to one person's opinion or one organization's priorities.
- If all your recognition comes from family, what happens when you need professional validation to negotiate a raise or apply for a leadership role?

Strong recognition portfolios draw from multiple sources. When one source temporarily dries up, as it may, you have others that can sustain you. It's a little bit like diversifying your investments: you wouldn't put all your money in one stock, so what would make you do the same when it comes to validation? From your list, identify one area where you'd like to seek more recognition or where you feel your efforts could be better acknowledged. Write down actionable steps for creating more opportunities for recognition in that area.

For example:

- **If work recognition is lacking:** Schedule a conversation with your manager about feedback frequency.
- **If external networks are absent:** Join one professional community, contribute your expertise online.
- **If self-recognition is minimal:** Start a weekly practice of writing down three things you're proud of regardless of whether anyone else noticed.

Key Points:

- **Recognition Is a Practice:** Recognition is the validation of who you are and how you are perceived. Be sure to keep the Shop open and have frequent visitors. Make adding to your Little Shop of Hoorays a weekly practice, not a one-time exercise.
- **Pay Attention to the Attention You Receive:** Recognition is only helpful if it's useful and specific. Be sure to ask for specific feedback.
- **Recognize Others:** It's an act that will fill you with joy and boost morale all around, so do it frequently.

- **It's All in the Praise:** What builds you up is what will fill your cup of contentment, so be sure to keep a log of all of these moments of positivity.
- **Small Wins Help You Sail Ahead:** Small wins are as important as big wins. Studies show that productivity increases along with recognition, so paying attention to all wins is critical.

PART III

OPPORTUNITIES: MAXIMIZING MOMENTS

Creating pathways for growth

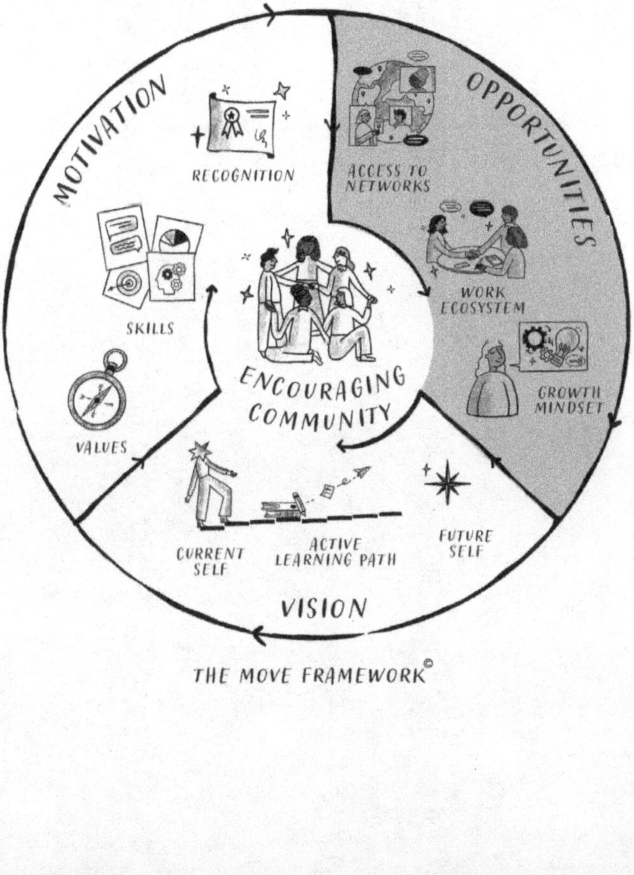

THE MOVE FRAMEWORK©

CHAPTER 8

OPTIMIZING OPPORTUNITIES

My friend Marina is a force of nature who could lead a masterclass in optimizing opportunities. She seizes the moment, any moment quite frankly, as much as she can wherever she can—not in a pushy way, but just because she's paying attention to her environment. She spots open doors everywhere. For example, if she's waiting to board a flight or at a bus stop, she will undoubtedly strike up a conversation, which has led to her meeting people who are still a part of her life today, people she can call true friends.

Often when I talk to clients, they have a narrow view as to what's possible, which makes perfect sense because that's precisely why we're meeting. The exploration of opportunities is a chance to open the aperture and close the fulfillment gap, that space between where you are now and where you want to be. Opportunities may not always be obvious, but they're around almost every corner.

Whether at church, your alumni group, or joining a sport or a class, there's no shortage of different ways to find opportunities. It's something even I have had to learn. When I realized that I'd lost touch with my college network, I rekindled those ties through LinkedIn and WhatsApp, which in turn led to all kinds of things (friendships, meaningful conversations, clients) that I would have never explored otherwise.

The part that I've noticed is the toughest for my clients is remaining open or vulnerable to receiving opportunities. How many times have you thought, "I can't possibly contact so-and-so…" and felt that inner ickiness? This is your scarcity mindset rearing its ugly head, and that internal chatter becomes an obstacle to seizing an opportunity with open arms. And there's another layer: You're so consumed with catering to everyone else's needs that stepping into the spotlight for yourself feels selfish.

So how do you move toward a place of abundance?

I have found three essential areas that women must tap into to open the door to opportunities:

1) **Being willing to access personal and professional networks**

   Accessing your networks is about strategic connection: the people you know and the people they know. It's about ensuring that you're a few degrees from someone who can help you, who can be in your corner. Women, who generally have wide networks, hesitate to tap into theirs for professional reasons fearing it may appear transactional, but it matters because everyone needs an active network.

2) **Taking stock of your work ecosystem**

   Your work ecosystem encompasses everything that impacts your workplace, from the content of your job, to your salary, to company culture, to your commute time. These factors shape your day-to-day experiences, influencing your job satisfaction and overall well-being. Women who have successfully designed their careers regularly take stock of their work and they stay abreast of factors that impact their life.

3) **Maintaining a growth mindset to stay the course even when the going gets tough**

   A growth mindset, perhaps the most critical of the three, means understanding that your abilities can develop through dedication and effort and viewing challenges as opportunities rather than obstacles. People who can embrace a growth mindset have the advantage of putting themselves in a place where they are primed for growth.

Mindset, the work ecosystem, and networks do not exist in isolation; rather, they reinforce each other. Your network helps you see possibilities, your work ecosystem helps you gauge what needs attention, and your growth mindset gives you the agency to act.

So, what does optimizing opportunities look like in practice?

It means going to events where you have a chance of meeting new people, whether it's your child's school potluck or a happy hour at the office. But it also means reaching out to your current network to check in regularly. It's often the people you don't expect who open the right doors. Mark Granovetter, a social scientist and professor at Stanford, is known for his research on the strength of "weak ties," which demonstrates how those you don't know as well, those outside of your immediate circle, are often the ones who offer new possibilities and new relationships. Practically speaking, your weak ties are your foot in the door. You're never going to know who may hold the key to your next big thing. It also means getting outside your comfort zone—taking a salsa class, training for a marathon, accepting your colleague's invitation to a girls' night out—because our closest friends and usual go-to activities aren't going to cut it when it comes to leveling up.

Fulfillment requires us to step into the spotlight for ourselves, being an active participant in our journeys. I've witnessed many talented women remain in roles that drain them, watching opportunities pass by, thinking "maybe someday" without ever taking action. Staying open to what may come and putting yourself in front of opportunities moves you from wishing to doing. It doesn't happen overnight, but it will get you in motion.

My friend Marina embodies all three essential areas for optimizing opportunities: Her network is vast and diverse, she's intentional about her work in the nonprofit sector, and her mindset keeps her constantly primed for new interactions.

In the next three chapters, we'll explore each of these areas in depth. You'll learn how to strategically access your networks without feeling guilty (chapter 9), audit your work ecosystem to identify what actually needs to change (chapter 10), and develop a growth mindset that keeps you resilient when challenges arise (chapter 11). We'll start with the area many women find simultaneously powerful and uncomfortable: accessing your networks. You'll learn not only where to find the people who could offer your next opportunity, but how to open yourself up to what will inevitably come your way if you know where to look for them.

CHAPTER 9

ACCESSING YOUR NETWORKS

Anita, a participant in my group coaching program, had a successful corporate career before taking time off to raise her two girls and later starting her own fashion-consulting business. The first time I met her I noticed her beauty above all else, her impeccable outfit, baggy jeans, a loose knit black sweater, and the fact that she resembles Halle Berry.

The group was also immediately drawn to Anita because she radiates warmth and kindness at every turn. She had recently relocated to the suburbs with her spouse and two teenagers, from a cozy two-bedroom in Hell's Kitchen to a three-bedroom house in a leafy suburb of Westchester.

In our initial session, when it was Anita's turn to introduce herself she was excited to tell the group about her move, but apprehensive about how she would initiate new friendships and new business connections in her new neighborhood. All her work and her clients had been in the city. Finding herself at a career crossroads, she had decided to join my coaching group, as she was debating whether to return to a full-time, in-house position or to reimagine her business now that she was no longer physically in the city. One thing was clear: She needed to find new clients pronto.

Her challenge? Her business was mainly referral-based and her clients were primarily in New York City. She knew she needed to start from scratch, reconnecting with people in her industry, but she didn't know how to go about it when she either hadn't seen them in a while or didn't have a specific reason to connect with them. She wanted her outreach to feel authentic, not transactional. She also didn't quite know who could help her nor what she would be asking of them. "I'd rather do a day's worth of ironing rather than reaching out to people," Anita told the group and we all laughed. Everyone understood how awkward it could be to reach out after years of no contact. We've all felt that dread around networking, and it's worth unpacking why it's never been anyone's favorite cup of tea. Anita's challenge is a common one: How do you access your network authentically?

WORKING YOUR NETWORK

You might associate networking with a gathering where you're standing around with a plastic cup of warm wine and a forced smile, as Anita did. But I'm talking about something different. There are many ways to access networks you already have ties to that don't include going to dreaded networking events (though we'll get to that too). As I told Anita, accessing your networks is about conversation catalysts.

99 Accessing your networks is about conversation catalysts.

A conversation catalyst is a natural spark, a question, observation, or shared moment, that can open a door to meaningful connection. Rather than scripted small talk, catalysts create authentic entry points for conversation that can reveal opportunities, or mutual interests. And often, these are hiding in plain sight: the person who asks a thoughtful question in a Zoom chat that sparks an idea, the friend who posts on LinkedIn about a career decision. The catalyst isn't your default wine-and-cheese mixer, it's a response to something that piques your interest.

It's usually when we least expect it that important conversations happen, which is why you need to be ready whether on the subway platform on your commute to work, at the check-out at Trader Joe's, in line for your coffee order, at school drop-off, in your doctor's waiting room, or at a book club—the list goes on. Wherever people gather, there's an opportunity for an unexpected conversation that can lead to the next big (or little) thing in your life.

These conversations are happening all the time, but you have to be willing to put yourself out there, to be bold, to tell others what you're looking for. When someone says, "how have you been?" you can say "fine," or you can say: "I've been working on that book/project/painting/poem/

song/[fill in the blank] that I've been dreaming about since I was a teenager," which may open up the conversation to an opportunity you may never have imagined.

In her book, *Build Like a Woman,* Kathleen Griffith calls these moments of manifesting "outrageous asks" and although, as she points out, most of them won't lead to anything, the ones that *will* will change your life. But that's the key. Your "ask" needs to be truly unreasonable. Truly transformational. Something you'd never imagine coming true. Maybe it's asking a friend to introduce you to Oprah. Or flying yourself to a conference so you can meet the exact person who can help you take your business to the next level. These are life-changing moves—if you're willing to be vulnerable and go after them.

The only way you're going to be able to have the version of the life you want is by pushing yourself out of your comfort zone. A no is simply a no *right now* or to this specific request. But it's also an opportunity to say: But what about this other thing? No is a redirection. It's a chance to close one door and open another.

Many women struggle because although we're excellent at building networks and supporting others, we're hesitant to actually use those networks for ourselves. We resist approaching others about things we need because it feels opportunistic, but the truth is networks thrive on reciprocity. When you reach out with curiosity and openness to a conversational exchange, you're actually strengthening your network for everyone. Accessing networks also means creating space to get to know someone better. Your networks are dynamic and forever changing. It's critical not to let them go stale.

As Minda Harts reminds us in *The Memo,* paying to be a part of events or networks where you can access those with shared affinities is a strategic use of your time and energy. "Use professional organizations or conferences to help you get in the rooms with the people you want to meet." It's not about collecting business cards, it's about positioning yourself in spaces where conversations and opportunities align with your work-life aspirations.

THE UPSIDE OF NETWORKING

The upside to accessing your networks is also about wellbeing. A number of studies show that positive, trusting relationships predict greater longevity and even a healthier life. In *The Lost Art of Connecting,* Susan McPherson shares how placing priority on building meaningful relationships leads to more fulfillment. As she has said in interviews, "If you make dedicating time, energy, to building meaningful connections a regular habit, it's as good as running every day and eating kale every day, in terms of your health and longevity."

When we nurture these connections, we're not just expanding professional contacts; we're creating communities that sustain us on all fronts. These connections provide joy, wisdom, and collective support: your daily kale salad of goodness. And it's not just who you know, but how you're connected (as was mentioned in Mark Granovetter's research on weak ties in chapter 8).

Building and tending to our networks is like planting a garden. You never know what will blossom. Whether you're seeking a new role or simply have an itch to explore something different, the impact of your network is not to be underestimated. If you underpin it with generosity, you will see that everyone benefits. As Keith Ferrazzi, author of *Never Eat Alone,* says: The key is to offer as much as you receive. But *who* do you need to get to know better and for *what purpose?*

WHO'S WHO AND WHAT FOR?

This is where it's important to know the distinction between two very specific types of relationships that women in particular benefit from: sponsors and mentors. A mentor gives advice and guidance. They're your sounding board for decisions and professional growth. But a sponsor helps advocate for you in rooms you're not in. Since women tend to self-promote less than men, having an advocate becomes crucial.

Carla Harris, who has spent thirty years as a vice chairman and managing director and who was appointed by former President Barack Obama to chair the National Women's Business Council, has written three leadership books and is also a gospel singer having sold out Carnegie Hall six times! In her book *Strategize to Win,* she writes about the key traits a sponsor should have: influence and social capital so they can recommend you for opportunities and open doors. Sponsors matter because people listen to them. Harris reveals that the trick to finding a sponsor is to study your organization for two weeks to identify the people with seats at decision-making tables.

Sponsors and mentors help you thrive because both help close your fulfillment gap, allowing you to gain visibility and access when you need it. And this isn't only about looking for the next promotion, it also means growing your own personal board of directors (or group of advisors), people whom you can count on not just in specific moments of need but who stay connected with you as your work life evolves.

For women of color, sponsors and mentors are even more critical because you'll likely need to forge relationships with leaders who don't look like you, since organizational power structures remain predominantly white and male. Research shows that similarity breeds connection, which means these relationships will take extra work as people gravitate toward those who remind them of themselves. Women of color lack access to mentors and sponsors: only 31 percent of entry-level women have sponsors compared to 45 percent of men. Women of color also face disparities in career-development opportunities—for instance, Black women receive stretch assignments at significantly lower rates (24 percent) compared to white women (35 percent). Women and particularly women of color can't rely on the same automatic connection that comes from shared experiences and backgrounds.

THE JOY OF NETWORKS

Studies show that we are hardwired for connection. In fact, our brains light up when we engage with others. Loneliness has measurable negative health effects, while meaningful connection literally extends our lives. When we talk about accessing networks, we're talking about finding people who inspire, energize, guide, support, and even make us laugh.

Some of the best professional connections can become genuine friendships. Your LinkedIn connection becomes your accountability partner for a creative project; that colleague from a few years back becomes your go-to for travel tips. We have to see those in our networks as whole people outside of what they can directly offer us. Oftentimes, we can't even imagine how someone can add value to our lives.

But don't push yourself to be someone you're not. Inauthenticity never works. Introverts, for example, can build powerful networks through deep one-on-one conversations. Extroverts can thrive in group settings and large events. Any approach works as long as you're working that network, joyfully and authentically.

UNDERSTANDING HOW NETWORKS WORK: THE KFC MODEL

Tapping our networks and who we know can be complex and intimidating. I started thinking about how to help my coaching clients sift through their networks and came up with a three-pronged approach I call the KFC model. This model helps you to map out your connections so that you have a better overview of who's in your orbit. Each letter stands for a type of person in your network:

Knowledge Holders: People who understand your field (or any field) and can provide expertise, information, and insights. They're the protein, your chicken thighs and wings, because they have substantive information that gives you solid direction and helps you grow.

Fans: Your cheerleaders and honest critics, friends, and peers who always have your back. They're your feel-good family, the comfort food, the coleslaw, the mashed potatoes and the biscuit.

Connectors: Similar to knowledge holders, the connectors are bridge-builders who know everyone and can open doors to new opportunities. They may not be specialists in your field, but their extensive networks make things happen. They are your sauces.

Of course, many people have multiple traits. Someone can be both a connector and a knowledge holder. The idea is to understand who plays what role in your network because that awareness helps you access the right people for the right reasons.

ANITA'S KFC ACTIVITY

Anita, who you will recall, had relocated to the suburbs, was eager to expand her network. She was already active in several communities as a member of a women's group and through sitting on the PTA of her daughters' high school. However, she hadn't actively tapped into those circles to seek opportunities.

I had her map out her professional network by identifying the three key KFC groups: knowledge-based connections who have the expertise she might be looking for; fans who support and champion her work; and connectors who may not be specialists in her field but have an extensive network.

Doing this exercise together, Anita identified thirty people whom she would contact from different buckets of connection in her life. We then explored what her specific "ask" was for each person. The discovery process included questions like:

- What do they know about her values?
- Do they know what she's looking for in her next role to feel fulfilled?
- Do they understand her skill set so they can help her find an opportunity that fits her strengths?
- We also sought to answer questions like: How could she be of help to each contact so the interaction felt useful on both sides and not transactional?

Anita found that having clarity around what she was searching for helped her become much more strategic about leveraging and nurturing old and new relationships. She observed that she was looking for connectors, people who could introduce her to new contacts in the fashion business. As a result, she successfully generated several new leads.

She not only attracted new client inquiries but secured new clients within a short time frame, giving her the confidence to fully commit to growing her business rather than returning to corporate life. The process gave her a much-needed confidence boost and reaffirmed her passion for what she was doing.

Finding fulfillment results from exploring the opportunities that are within reach. And these opportunities come from exposure and connection. The more you seek out opportunities and raise your hand to pursue them, the better chance you have of finding one that brings you fulfillment. Instead of approaching a closed door, your network knocks on those doors for you.

But if you don't have access to networks, or you've let connections go, how do you reactivate those relationships? It's about the intention and the approach. When Anita asked people for just fifteen minutes of their time they overwhelmingly said yes. Reaching out is not an imposition; it's an invitation to connection.

Now it's your turn.

ACTIVITY: YOUR KFC BUCKET

Get a sheet of paper and a pen and, if you can, get a few Post-its too. Create three columns on your paper and label them:

Knowledge Holders (the protein: experts with substance)

Fans (the comfort sides: your cheerleaders)

Connectors (the bridge-builders: door-openers)

Set a ten-minute timer and write down the names of people in your professional orbit. Be sure to include current and former colleagues, managers, mentors, clients, professional contacts, and LinkedIn connections that you have interacted with on more than one occasion.

Aim for at least twenty to thirty names.

Now put them into one (or more) buckets by asking:

Knowledge Holders: Who has the expertise I need? Who is extremely knowledgeable in my field or an adjacent field?

Fans: Who celebrates my wins? Who gives me honest feedback? Who do I call when I need encouragement?

Connectors: Who seems to know everyone? Who has introduced me to people before? Who always says "Oh, you should meet…"?

If someone fits multiple categories, list them in the bucket that's most useful to you right now.

Now look at your buckets:

KFC MODEL

KNOWLEDGE HOLDERS

FANS

CONNECTORS

WHICH BUCKET IS FULLEST? WHICH IS EMPTIEST? WHICH NEEDS A REFILL?

DO I HAVE ENOUGH CONNECTORS, FANS OR KNOWLEDGE HOLDERS TO SUPPORT ME?

WHO WILL I SPEAK TO?

- Which bucket is the fullest? Which is emptiest? Which needs a refill?
- Do I have enough connectors, fans, or knowledge holders to support me at this moment?
- Can you speak to someone in each of the buckets? And can you share something that will help that person?

HOW MEN AND WOMEN USE NETWORKS DIFFERENTLY

Research by Herminia Ibarra, a professor of organizational behavior at London Business School, shows us that men and women use networks differently. Men typically have other men in their networks and use those connections instrumentally to access opportunities and advance careers. Women generally take a two-pronged approach: seeking *instrumental access* (career advancement, opportunities) from men and *social support* (encouragement, advice) from women.

This isn't inherently problematic, but it can limit you. If you only build deep emotional networks with other women without cultivating instrumental connections, knowledge holders, and connectors, you miss out on opportunities. Why? Because your close friends typically know the same people and information you do. To make use of your network to the fullest, it's also important to activate your weak ties as we discussed earlier. Weak ties connect you to different circles, bringing introductions you'd not otherwise have.

For women specifically, these weak ties are particularly powerful, and research from the *Academy of Management*

Journal shows that while women are 40 percent less likely than men to form strong ties with senior leaders through direct interactions, they're actually better than men at building high-status networks when they leverage introductions through mutual contacts.

VALERIE'S STORY

I was sitting in a brightly lit women's coworking space waiting for Valerie, who had been referred to me because she wanted to leave banking after eighteen years in the industry. It was the first time we were meeting in person, even though we had had a few sessions online, and I spotted her right away when she walked into the lobby. She had her backpack hanging off one shoulder and pen and paper already clasped in her hand.

Prior to meeting up, we had decided to spend the session mapping out her network with the use of Post-its, crayons, pens, and flipcharts, as she had come with the specific intention to work on how to better access her network. She reminded me that she had basically been head down, deep in work for the last almost two decades, as a software engineer in a bank, working full time, as was her husband, and raising three children under the age of eight. She had remained inactive on LinkedIn and as a deep introvert didn't have the desire to make any changes.

But after so long, Valerie found herself finally ready to explore new opportunities. When I checked, though, she only had fifty connections on LinkedIn. Having spent her whole career at one company, her network was small, and it revolved around work colleagues and her circle of friends, primarily other parents on the PTA. Now she was faced with a dilemma: She wanted to move into AI, but how? Did anyone she knew have contacts in the industry? Could she speak to someone who currently worked in machine learning to see if it was something she'd enjoy?

Valerie's situation illustrates why weak ties matter. She needed to reactivate dormant connections (former classmates, old colleagues) and build bridges to new circles in the AI and machine-learning space. So, we started with baby steps. First, through LinkedIn, she identified former colleagues now working in AI. Then she reached out to acquaintances from past jobs she'd lost touch with. She also joined an online community focused on AI. Each week, her goal was just three actions:

1.) Reconnect with one person she hadn't spoken to in at least a year.

2.) Engage meaningfully in one online discussion.

3.) Reach out to one new person for a fifteen-minute informational conversation.

Within two months, Valerie had had a number of phone calls and her connections grew significantly. More importantly, she'd built confidence in her ability to have professional conversations and realized that most people were genuinely happy to help when asked. The network she thought didn't exist had been absent, but she was able to revive it. And she learned a tremendous amount from former colleagues, friends of friends, and even had some short consultancies offered to her. She ultimately chose to go back to university to complete a one-year course in AI, something that gave her much joy and satisfaction.

Not everyone will see such strong results right away, but making the move into growing your network is the first step to the change you want to see.

HOW TO MAKE AN ASK

This is the moment when you might be wondering: How do I ask my network for help? When reaching out, focus on three elements:

- **Be specific about what you're looking for and clarify your intention:** "I'm exploring a transition from corporate law to non-profit leadership" or "I'm curious about how you built your consulting practice after leaving in-house roles." The more specific you are, the easier you make it for someone to be helpful.
- **Make the ask small and time-bound:** Fifteen minutes for one piece of advice. When you respect people's time and make the commitment clear, they're more likely to engage.
- **Think about reciprocity from the beginning:** How can this be useful for both of you? Maybe you can offer an introduction, share an article relevant to their work, or simply bring a fresh perspective from your industry. Even if you can't offer something immediately, expressing genuine interest in their journey, and not just what they can do for you, creates an authentic exchange.

Of course, not every connection will respond, and that's okay. People are busy with life. Send one thoughtful message. If you don't hear back in a week or two, you could send one brief follow-up. After that, let it go gracefully. Remember, it's a numbers game. Celebrate the connections that do happen rather than dwelling on the ones that don't.

Accessing your networks is about engaging and nurturing your growing community in a way that feels sustainable and joyful. Add a calendar reminder to remember to reach out to those who have helped you. Close the loop by sharing how they made a difference to you. It's just as important to maintain your network once it's activated.

Now it's your turn.

ACTIVITY: REVIEW YOUR NETWORK

Answer yes or no to the following questions:

- Are your instrumental connections, knowledge holders, and connectors diverse in seniority, industry, and identity?
- Are you relying solely on close friends for job information, are your weak ties all in the same circle?
- Do you have access to decision-makers within your network?

If you answered no to question 1: Cultivate relationships with people from different departments, levels, backgrounds, and industries.

If you answered no to question 2: Reconnect with former colleagues, classmates, or acquaintances to activate those weak ties!

If you answered no to question 3: Look for opportunities for more visibility. For example, join professional associations, volunteer for roles (PTA, nonprofit boards), attend industry conferences, or participate in projects in-house.

If you answered no to most or all of the questions, start with one action this week. Pick the easiest connection to reactivate or the most accessible opportunity. You likely already have networks you're not fully leveraging: high school or college alumni, your neighbors, your children's school, professional associations, even your local coffee shop regulars. The invitation is to expand your footprint beyond comfortable circles where everyone looks and thinks like you.

Key Points:

- **Fill Your KFC Bucket:** Identify your knowledge holders, fans, and connectors. Audit where you have gaps and fill them intentionally.
- **Weak Ties Offer Strong Opportunities:** Your acquaintances and dormant connections (former colleagues, classmates) often provide more novel opportunities than close friends because they connect you to different circles. Not everyone will respond, and that's normal. Follow up where you can and let go gracefully when people don't respond.

- **Seek Sponsors and Mentors:** Mentors guide you; sponsors advocate for you in rooms you're not in. Both matter, but sponsors are often the missing piece for women's advancement. Identify someone senior with influence who can support your career trajectory.
- **Give It Your All:** Maintain your network by consistently sharing articles, making introductions, celebrating wins, and engaging with others' content. Small, consistent gestures build lasting relationships.
- **Guilt No More:** Reaching out isn't opportunistic when it's authentic and reciprocal. You strengthen networks by activating them, not by staying silent. Strategic networking transforms feeling opportunistic into feeling empowered.

CHAPTER 10

WORK ECOSYSTEM: OPTIMIZING YOUR WORKPLACE DYNAMICS

I didn't recognize the number, so I let it go straight to voicemail. It turns out it was Chiara, a participant in one of my autumn career events at Soho House. There were just over twenty midcareer professionals in that session, all braving the rain for a workshop on how to elevate their careers. But Chiara stood out because she made a beeline to a front-row seat (no one ever sits in the front row voluntarily!) and she came with an array of crayons, ready to take copious notes because, as she told me later, she wanted to focus and not be distracted by anyone. Now here she was, reaching out eight weeks later because she had had an aha moment during the event and wanted to share what had transpired since the workshop.

When I listened to her message I called her back right away and we planned an in-person meet up. She showed up the following week at Luminary, a coworking space in midtown Manhattan with her crumpled activity sheet, and on it was scribbled a pie chart that outlined her work ecosystem. "I carry this worksheet in my handbag every day!" she told me, and we both laughed as we hugged hello.

Chiara was an events manager who worked for a small co-working space in New York City, but she had been feeling less than fulfilled lately and was ready to quit the events business altogether. She didn't have a backup plan, though, nor the financial means to take such a leap. But she was deeply frustrated with her work life and had run out of ideas on next steps. She had joined my session because she wanted help.

The other participants that night were in similar situations: lost and looking to brainstorm about their work life. You don't attend a career workshop because you have it all figured out. It's usually because you're looking for inspiration and a kick in the pants. But what I tried to explain to Chiara and the others at the event that night was that it's usually not your entire job that's the problem. More often than not, it's a few aspects that are the issue, which is why the work ecosystem audit is a way to pinpoint the problem with intention.

Your Work Ecosystem

National Geographic defines the ecosystem as "a geographic area where plants, animals, and other organisms, as well as weather and landscapes, work together to form a bubble of life." Just as a natural ecosystem thrives when all its elements work in harmony, your work ecosystem does the same.

Think of your work ecosystem as the bubble of your work life, composed of your colleagues, your team, the organizational culture, physical environment, location, and all other elements that impact your workplace (from the content of your job to your commute time). These elements shape your day-to-day experiences, influencing your work life satisfaction and overall well-being.

But typically my clients just focus on one aspect of their work and use that as a gauge for all that is wrong with their jobs, basing their decisions on a fraction of the full picture.

I use the work ecosystem pie as a way to slow the conversation down and explore the root cause of their dissatisfaction. I've also customized the pie to reflect industry-specific areas. Here is a sample work ecosystem:

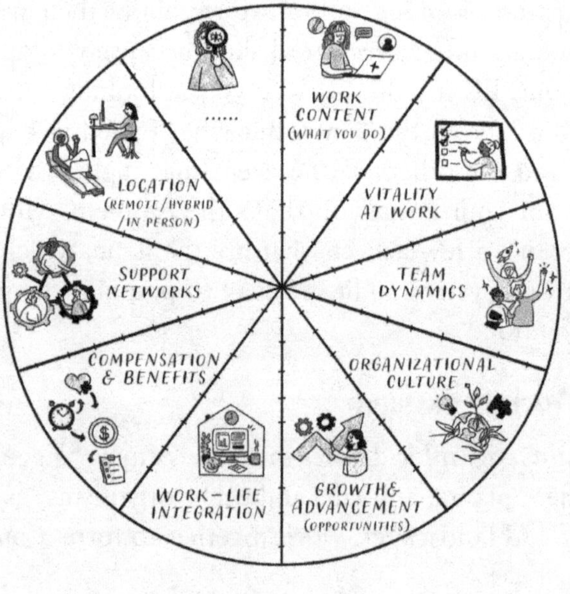

Think of each slice as a dimension of your work experience that makes up your complete work life picture. The idea is to rate your level of satisfaction in each slice of the pie from a scale of 1 (dissatisfied) to 10 (fully satisfied) to better understand what needs attention.

Here are the ten slices in more detail:

- **Team Dynamics:** Whether you are working in a team or solo, this is about the level of collaboration, support, and communication you experience in your work environment. It's about whether you feel heard, valued, and connected to the people you work with.
- **Work Content: What You Do**: These are your primary focus areas—the core of *what* you're responsible for delivering and *why*. As Dr. Ella F. Washington reminds us in *Unspoken,* your work is always more than a job description—you have the opportunity to create your own niche by going beyond what's expected and adding unique value.
- **Vitality at Work:** This is about how the work itself affects your energy—whether it energizes or depletes you, creates flow or feels draining. Does it make you lose track of time or watch the clock?
- **Growth and Advancement:** These are the opportunities to expand your skill set and knowledge, whether through formal learning, skill development, or taking on new challenges. This could be access to training or taking on a stretch assignment.
- **Work-Life Integration:** This is where work and life co-exist. People often refer to this slice as work-life

balance. At the end of the day we're trying to integrate work into our lives so it doesn't cannibalize all of our time and energy. This includes your schedule flexibility, boundary-setting, and whether your work rhythm accommodates your personal commitments.

- **Compensation and Benefits:** The compensation or rewards you receive, not only in terms of salary but any benefits such as, educational grants, maternity leave, health coverage, and pension plan.
- **Organizational Culture:** Whether you're a solopreneur or work in an organization, this is the energy and vibe that turns your environment into a space you enjoy working in.
- **Location:** This relates to where you work geographically, whether in person, remote or both.
- **Support Networks:** These networks are made up of those individuals who support you in times of need, be it in the workspace or outside of work.
- **Blank:** This is your opportunity to fill in the blank. It's the slice you create based on what matters uniquely to you. This might be, for example, health and wellness, volunteering, or other areas that are not captured in your work-life pie but that matter to you.

CHIARA'S PIE

Once we ordered, Chiara pulled out her work-ecosystem worksheet and placed it on the table in front of us. She glanced over at the pie and pointed to Work Content as the first category she wanted to explore. "I started with work content because that's what I thought was the problem," but when she gave it a score she quickly pegged it as an 8/10, which meant she felt pretty satisfied in that area. She loved planning events, the creative problem-solving involved in bringing people together, and the satisfaction of executing unique spaces where professionals made meaningful connections.

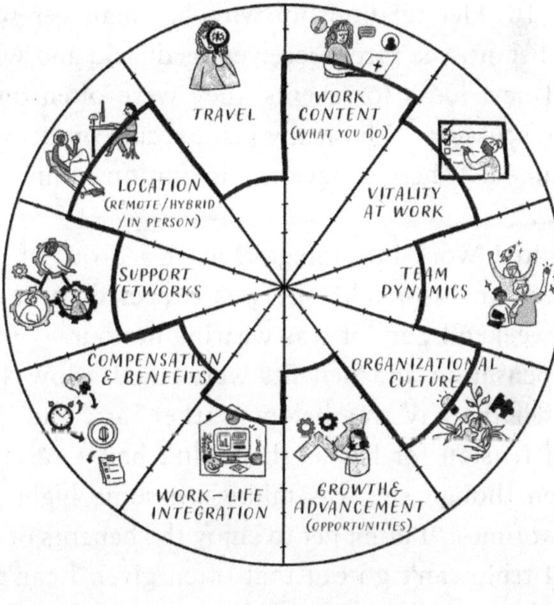

She didn't rate the slices in any particular order; she simply went with whatever drew her attention. Vitality at Work she rated 7 out of 10—not terrible, but not where she wanted it to be. While she enjoyed most of her daily activities, the administrative burden was heavier than she wanted. The email influx was eating up her time and she was tethered to her phone at all hours. "I'm drained and drowning in emails, and I'm glued to my phone 24/7," she said when I asked her what was keeping that 7 from being an 8 or 9.

Next was Growth and Advancement, which she ranked a 3 out of 10. "There is literally no advancement opportunity in this company," she told me, which she found "so depressing." Her small co-working space had no senior events role, no learning budget, and her manager showed minimal interest in her development. She was at a dead end.

Team Dynamics was only slightly better. She rated it a 5 out of 10. Her relationship with her manager was cordial but distant. She rarely received feedback, and when she proposed new ideas for events, they were often dismissed without discussion. "I basically just execute on her orders," she explained. "There is never an invitation to initiate anything new."

She rated Work-Life Integration at a 5 out of 10. The hours were unreasonable; she was expected to be on call through weekends, and it was wearing her out.

Compensation and Benefits were rated a low 4 out of 10. She felt the pay was below market rate, and it was a source of tension for her as she hadn't had a raise in two years even though she was taking on some higher-profile projects at times. "I don't get to enjoy the benefits of the city because I truly can't go out that often given I can't afford it," she told me. "I have turned down evenings with friends because I'm embarrassed that I don't make enough money to eat out." Next Chiara rated the Organizational Culture a 7 out of 10. The co-working space had a friendly, casual vibe, and she was aligned with the values and vibe of the company.

She loved working in Manhattan, and the commute from Brooklyn was manageable. She was happy to rate the Location an 8 out of 10.

She reflected on her Support Networks and ranked them a 6 out of 10. Chiara had a few colleagues she enjoyed but no real mentors or anyone she could turn to for support. Outside of work, she had friends in the industry, but no one who she felt could directly help her advance.

She chose Travel as the theme for her blank category, and she rated it a 4 out of 10. She didn't get to travel anywhere for very long and had primarily enjoyed long weekends in upstate New York. She was longing to visit the Caribbean but didn't have enough days off nor the means to take a vacation outside the US.

Seeing the visual representation of her pie was an eye opener for her. "I kept telling myself I hated my job and wanted to change fields," she told me as we sipped our tea. "But looking at the pie, I realized I don't hate what I do as much as feel deeply frustrated with being underpaid and not recognized for my efforts."

That clarity helped her brainstorm what she needed to do to close her fulfillment gap. It wasn't leaving the industry; it was looking for another organization, where compensation was better aligned with her expectations and where there was opportunity for growth.

On a bleak rainy afternoon, about five months later, I got a text from Chiara, in all caps: "I GOT A JOB!!!!" followed by a line of laughing emojis. She had secured a role as an events manager at a larger co-working company with multiple locations. They had growth opportunities and a better pay and benefits package. She was still at the same level but there were opportunities for advancement. Her pie looked dramatically different in her new role.

Chiara's experience isn't unique. I've seen how insights from the work ecosystem exercise move clients to action.

Take Carol, a financial analyst at a mid-sized firm, for example. She was trying to figure out a better work-life setup. She had low ratings in both work-life integration and health and wellness because of her long commute, which meant she didn't have time to go to the gym or relax at the end of the day. She rarely did anything outside of her job. After working through her work-life pie, she negotiated one remote day per week, which gave her the chance to arrange sports activities that she could fit in just after her workday on the days she worked from home. She also made it clear to her boss and colleagues that she wouldn't answer after-hours emails. While it didn't fix everything, these changes made her work life much more sustainable. In addition, once she had started exercising again, it gave her the energy and confidence to exercise on the weekends too, something she had been avoiding for a long time. She started bringing this renewed momentum into more areas of her life.

While Chiara needed to leave her role to find more fulfillment, Carol was able to look at her work ecosystem and make small tweaks that changed everything for her.

WHY IT MATTERS

Given that you will spend approximately eighty thousand working hours in your career (forty years times fifty weeks times forty hours), understanding your work ecosystem isn't just nice to have, it's essential for your fulfillment.

> **Understanding your work ecosystem isn't just nice to have, it's essential for your fulfillment.**

It doesn't help that Harvard Business School research found that the average workday has increased by 8.2 percent, an extra 48.5 minutes per day, with people working all hours, especially as boundaries between work and personal time blur. Your ecosystem is either sustaining your work life or slowly wearing you down. Which is it for you?

Now let's explore your work ecosystem pie. Be sure to define the significance of each slice. For example, location might be something that's extremely important to you because you need the flexibility to work from home. For someone else, location could be the desire to work in a specific city or country. Two different perceptions of what an ideal location setup might be, but an important distinction to make.

Another area I see a lot of differences around is company culture. Some people want a fast-paced, competitive environment, while others prefer a feeling of inclusion and belonging. Your work ecosystem pie isn't one-size-fits-all. It's unique to you.

ACTIVITY: YOUR WORK ECOSYSTEM PIE

As you audit your own work ecosystem, take the time to explore each slice with a critical lens. You might be wondering where to start and whether to take a leap but oftentimes, the main question is really: Does this work ecosystem support my aspirations? If the answer is no, then you need to look more carefully at what needs to change.

Your work ecosystem pie is both a diagnostic tool and a conversation starter. This activity is also useful for managers who want to have career discussions with their direct reports, as it creates a shared language around what fulfillment looks like in the workplace. You can use it with someone you manage or you can use it on your own. Either way, by observing your level of satisfaction, you have the ability to see how to close your fulfillment gap.

To help you rank each slice, you can reflect on these sample questions to help you assess your current satisfaction level within your ecosystem.

Work Content (What You Actually Do Each Day)

- What would you tell someone if they asked you to describe what you actually do all day?
- What types of work take up most of your time, and in what proportions?
- If you could redesign your role, what responsibilities would you keep, add, or remove?

Vitality at Work (Energy and Engagement with Your Tasks)

- If you could spend 80 percent of your time on one type of work, what would it be?
- What task or project has made you lose track of time recently?
- What would need to change for you to feel more vitality in your daily work?

Growth and Advancement (Learning and Progression Opportunities)

- When was the last time you learned something new at work?
- What does your path forward look like in your current role or organization?
- Where do you see yourself twelve months from now?

Team Dynamics (Quality of Relationships and Collaboration)

- How would you describe your relationship with your manager and colleagues?
- Who do you turn to when you need support at work?
- What do you enjoy/dislike most about the team dynamics?

Work-Life Integration

- How often do you work outside your intended hours?
- When was the last time work prevented you from doing something personally important?
- How do you feel at the end of a typical workday?

Compensation and Benefits

- How do you feel about your current compensation?
- What financial stress, if any, does your current salary create?

- What benefits matter most to you that you're either getting or missing?

Organizational Culture

- What three words would you use to describe your workplace culture?
- How are mistakes handled in your organization?
- When you think about the culture, does it energize or exhaust you?

Location

- How well does your current work arrangement (remote/office/hybrid) match your needs?
- How does your commute or workspace affect your energy and productivity?
- What would your ideal work location or setup look like?

Support Networks (Your circle inside and outside work)

- Who are your allies at work—people you trust and who advocate for you?
- When you're struggling, who do you reach out to and what kind of support do they provide?
- How satisfied are you with the professional support you have? What about the personal support?

Other (Your custom slice)

- What would bring you fulfillment that hasn't been named yet? For example, health and wellness, meaningful impact, travel, caregiving setup.

Rating Your Pie:

Once you've given a rating to each of your ecosystem slices, look at your scores.

Slices that you rated 1–4: High priority. These areas are actively depleting you and likely contributing to stress, burnout, or dissatisfaction. These are your priority slices.

Slices that you rated 5–6: The in-between. These areas are not supporting you as well as they could and should be your secondary focus areas.

Slices that you rated 7–10: Go with the flow. These areas are sources of satisfaction and should be maintained or celebrated.

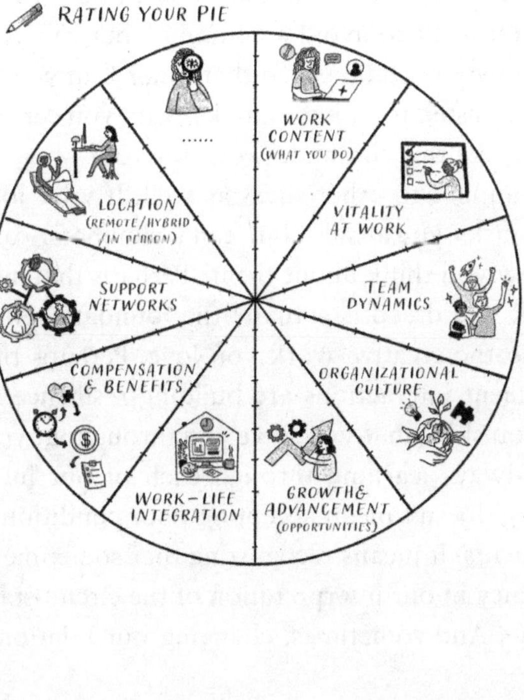

When multiple slices rate equally low, start with the one that, if improved, would have the greatest ripple effect on the others. For example, improving team dynamics often positively impacts your job satisfaction overall.

The moment you observe the shift you want to make is not the same moment that change will occur. The important part is to stay the course and to keep your aspiration in the forefront of your mind.

THE REFRAME

Sometimes, the gap isn't about changing your circumstances, it's about reframing them. For example, if commute time is rated low, you can ask yourself: How do I learn to accept the current setup and even, dare I say, find meaning in it? Maybe you want to avoid a commute, but can you instead explore how you could spend that time? Can you find some podcasts to listen to or audiobooks? Can you carpool? How can you make this commute work for you?

This applies to other slices as well. If your job content includes tasks you dislike but can't eliminate, can you reframe how you think about them? Perhaps that administrative work you dread is actually the foundation that allows you to do the creative work you love. Perhaps those challenging client interactions are building resilience and communication skills that will serve you throughout your career. We are always learning through each of our interactions. Reframing doesn't mean accepting poor conditions or toxic environments. It means recognizing that sometimes we have more agency in our interpretation of the circumstances than we realize. And sometimes, changing our relationship to a situation can shift our experience of it significantly. We will discuss this in the next chapter on mindset.

STAYING PUT

I want to acknowledge that not everyone reading this book has the flexibility or resources to make immediate larger changes to their work ecosystem. Perhaps you're on a visa that ties you to your current employer or you're the primary breadwinner. Or perhaps you're caring for family members and can't risk any disruption to your income or healthcare. Or perhaps you're in a field with limited opportunities in your geographic area.

If you're in a situation where external changes aren't possible right now, the work ecosystem pie is still valuable. It helps you to:

Name what's happening. Naming the problem helps you to normalize what you're experiencing, and it also helps you to share your story. It's likely that others have experienced what you're going through in your work life.

Validate your experience. When you can see your scores, both low and high, you have evidence that your job isn't all bad or all good, but somewhere in between.

Protect what you can. Even if you can't change jobs, you might be able to set small boundaries, cultivate support networks inside and outside of work, or reframe certain aspects of your situation. These micro-adjustments can make a difficult situation more tolerable. If you're struggling with significant stress related to your work situation, please know that support exists. Mental health support groups—many free and virtual—can be a valuable first step.

Be ready to make changes when needed. Knowing which slices need attention means that when a window of opportunity appears you'll know what to prioritize to give you more satisfaction.

Revisit Your Pie. Your work ecosystem is dynamic, not static. Life changes, priorities shift, organizations evolve or stagnate. I would recommend revisiting your work ecosystem pie every six to twelve months, to take stock of what has shifted. Regular check-ins with your ecosystem help you stay proactive. They help you notice the issues that may creep in and also remind you to celebrate when things are going well. The pie isn't a one-time assessment; it's a tool you should return to throughout your work life.

Key Points:

- **Each Slice Has a Price.** Like Chiara, you might discover that it's not your entire job that's the problem, but specific slices of your work ecosystem. Identifying which slices need attention prevents you from making hasty decisions that uproot your entire life when targeted changes could help close your fulfillment gap.
- **Health Is a Priority.** With workplace stress on the rise as well as employee burnout, optimizing your work ecosystem isn't a luxury; it's a survival strategy. Those eighty thousand-plus hours you'll spend

working over your career are hours that shouldn't take on an unbalanced amount of your energy and well-being.

- **Reclaim Your Reframe.** Sometimes the solution isn't changing your circumstances but changing how you relate to them. Whether it's transforming your commute into learning time or having a career conversation with your manager, reframing allows you to explore opportunities.
- **Be Ready for the Ripple Effect.** Like Chiara discovered, improving one low-scoring slice can create a ripple effect throughout your entire ecosystem. Look for those leverage points.
- **Pinpoint Your Pain Point.** You can't optimize every slice of your work ecosystem simultaneously, but by identifying your lowest-ranking slices and focusing your energy there, you can close your fulfillment gap and create a work life that sustains rather than depletes you.

Taking the time to closely monitor your work ecosystem helps identify where fulfillment thrives and where it falters. As Chiara discovered that rainy evening at Soho House, the "I quit" knee-jerk response is not always necessary. Sometimes it's about paying closer attention to what actually needs fixing. Auditing her work ecosystem made her see what was no longer serving her and more importantly, what it was that she was actually after so that she could articulate it better. It also helped her see where things were going well and where she needed to gain more joy in her work life. That's the power of creating your own pie.

CHAPTER 11

YOUR MINDSET IS YOUR GREATEST ASSET

In the previous chapters we explored how to access your network and audit your work ecosystem. Yet even with the knowledge of who can help you and what needs to change, there's one essential piece that will determine how you move forward, and that is your mindset.

There's a famous quote from Henry Ford, "Whether you think you can, or you think you can't, you're right," and I've found this to be an essential truth in my work. Ask yourself: Are you the type that tells yourself that you can? That even if you don't know how to do something that you'll figure it out? Or are you one of those people who's constantly using the word *can't:*

- I can't get promoted
- I can't change careers
- I can't write a book
- I can't start my own company

That single word—can't—can become the barrier to joy and hope.

Psychologist Carol Dweck calls this the fixed mindset, and her research explains why a fixed mindset is so detrimental. In her book *Mindset: The New Psychology of Success,* she shows us that we all carry two competing narratives: the fixed mindset that says our abilities are set in stone, and the growth mindset that believes we can develop through effort and learning. In other words, there's a part of you that believes you can learn, grow, and develop new capabilities (growth mindset), and the part that whispers, rather incessantly, "it's never going to work out" (fixed mindset).

I call these static versus dynamic mindsets. A static mindset keeps us where we are, stuck in our current narrative about what we can and cannot do, while a dynamic mindset propels us forward, adapting and responding to what life throws our way. The point isn't whether you have a negative mindset at times; we all do. The question is whether you're willing to notice when it shows up and decide it doesn't get the final say.

THE MIND DETERMINES THE MOVE

Here's a recurring theme I hear in women's circles: Many of us talk about that silent yet steady voice of "not possible, too difficult, won't happen, not going to work, no, not now, and never." Your brain is wired to keep you comfortable, to pay more attention to threats and negative experiences than positive ones. And there is often a chorus of friends and family at the ready to confirm your safe choices. As well-meaning as they are, they often say things like, "You've got a great thing going, why would you want to change things up?" Their words feel like support, but often, they just echo your own static mindset that wants you to avoid risk. Yet playing it safe is its own hazard. Because with security comes a minimizing mindset that tells you to keep your life small and controlled. And in that space, you are left joyless and without fulfillment.

Our brains aren't trying to sabotage us; they're trying to protect us. The human brain has what neuroscientists call a "negativity bias," a survival mechanism that kept our ancestors alive and alert. As psychologist Rick Hanson explains, our brains are "Velcro for negative experiences, Teflon for positive ones." We're wired to remember the one criticism in a sea of praise, to focus on what could go wrong rather than what might go right.

The negativity bias doesn't only affect how you process experiences; it shapes what you even allow yourself to consider. When an opportunity appears that could bring you more joy, your brain checks for threats, for discomfort, and you may end up talking yourself out of exploring the possibility before you even get started.

But remember, even with a dynamic mindset, real setbacks hurt. Sometimes talking yourself through tough situations isn't enough; you need rest, a community, an opportunity to weigh your options.

BINA'S STORY

Bina is a classic example of having a static mindset. Bina's first words out of her mouth when I met her on our first video session were: "I don't stand a chance of getting a promotion four months post–maternity leave. I can't even see how I would position myself." Bina, who had been working for a nonprofit for three years before having her baby, had recently returned from maternity leave and found herself feeling disconnected from work, torn between proving herself professionally and being a present parent. She feared that her time away from the office had left her "out of favor" and unsure about current projects. Although she wanted to explore new opportunities, she hesitated, worrying that it might put her job at risk. She was telling me that she had no chance, that it just wouldn't happen because she hadn't seen anyone else do it, and she didn't want to ask for more because she should be grateful her job was still there. Her own static beliefs were keeping her in a negative frame of mind.

Her mother in particular, whom she was very close to, encouraged her to stay silent and appreciate her job. "You've worked so hard to get to where you are," her mother reminded her. "It's better to stay with what you know than what you think you might get" was another. And then of course, "When I was your age, I didn't rock the boat, I was simply grateful to be employed."

Bina's internal chatter came disguised as a variety of characters. Tara Mohr, author of *Playing Big,* distinguishes between our "inner critic" (the voice of internalized criticism) and our "inner mentor" (our wisest self), reminding us that we can choose which voice to amplify as we grow. Shirzad Chamine, in his work on *Positive Intelligence,* calls our internal chatter our saboteurs, our negative voices that undermine confidence and self-worth, often manifesting as self-doubt. Think of your saboteurs as the chatterbox that's taking center stage. The first step is recognizing when they're speaking.

Bina's chatterbox was loud and insistent. She didn't feel she could add value or be considered seriously as a working parent. During our coaching conversations, we started tracking the patterns of her thoughts: what she was telling herself and what was triggering them. She began to notice that she would default to a static mindset. Her fear was taking over.

Unfortunately, Bina's story isn't unique. Many women discover that their real obstacle isn't capability, it's fear. But what are they afraid of?

Some of the most common fears that I've seen regardless of background, industry or seniority are:

- **Fear of visibility.** For many women, staying small means staying safe from scrutiny, from criticism, from the tall poppy syndrome that cuts down women who stand out. One acquaintance told me, "If I take that VP role, everyone will be watching. What if I fail?" She'd been succeeding publicly for years, but now she worried that she'd fall flat on her face.

- **Fear of being "found out."** Imposter syndrome whispers, "You don't really belong here" and gets louder as opportunities get bigger. It's when you convince yourself that you have fooled people into thinking you're competent and that someone is about to find out.
- **Fear of imperfection.** There's a perfectionist streak that gets in our way. It tells us: "I need to be 100 percent ready before I apply for that role" or "I should wait until I've mastered this particular thing before I throw my hat in the ring." But studies show that men apply for jobs when they meet 60 percent of the qualifications, while women wait until they meet 100 percent!
- **Fear of disappointing others.** Many women carry an invisible weight born from the roles and responsibilities we carry and the perceived impact of our choices on others. "If I change careers, what about my team? What about my family's expectations? What if I let people down?" This fear keeps you tethered to roles that no longer fit out of loyalty to everyone except yourself.

Any of these fears, individually or together, create a static mindset that keeps us stuck and unfulfilled.

SETTING YOUR MINDSET

You can have a perfectly mapped work ecosystem, knowing exactly what energizes you and what drains you. You can have access to a powerful network of people who could open doors. But if your mindset filters out opportunities before they can become real possibilities, you'll be unable to move toward work that could fulfill you.

> **If your mindset filters out opportunities before they can become real possibilities, you'll be unable to move toward work that could fulfill you.**

The static mindset curbs your approach to trying something new. "I'm not a networker" becomes "networking isn't an option to consider." "I'm not a leader" means you don't see yourself in leadership opportunities.

Your mindset shapes what you perceive as possible. Barbara Fredrickson, a psychology professor and pioneering researcher in positive emotions, developed the influential "broaden-and-build" theory that explains how positive emotions expand our thinking, creativity, and ability to see possibilities—and consequently access more joy and fulfillment. A static mindset creates tunnel vision where we only notice risks and find reasons why we shouldn't do something.

The first step to shifting your static mindset is becoming aware of it. Your inner chatter runs on repeat, like bad elevator music. You want to tune that out and focus on your dynamic mindset. The dynamic mindset is a joy lever for opportunity and exploration.

Mindset is what transforms knowledge into action, and possibility into practice. The women who find more joy and fulfillment in their work life aren't the ones who had perfect circumstances or lucky breaks. They're the ones who decided, "Why not me?" when opportunity showed up. They're the ones who said, "I don't know how yet, but I can figure it out." They're the ones who felt scared and moved forward anyway.

Your mind decides for you, but you get to decide what you tell your mind. You get to choose which story you put into practice, which narrative you lead with, and which possibilities you allow yourself to consider.

The question isn't whether you can or can't. The question is: What becomes possible when you believe that you can?

WATCH YOUR WORDS

Just as Bina started our conversation with "I'm not good at...," notice the phrases that aren't helpful in your exploration.

- **I can't:** I can't do public speaking, I can't start over....
- **That's not for me:** That role isn't for someone like me, that industry isn't for people with my background....
- **It's too late:** I'm too old, I've been out of the workforce too long....
- **I don't have:** I don't have the right degree, the right connections....

When you hear yourself using this language, pause and ask: Is this fact or feelings?

If you find yourself ruling things out before you've even explored them, that's your static mindset at work telling you it's not the right time or you have to wait for permission. Instead, build awareness by asking yourself these questions:

- What opportunities have I dismissed this week/ month without considering them?
- What did I tell myself about why they weren't for me?
- When do I most strongly hear the "I can't" voice?

ACTIVITY: THE POSSIBILITY PIVOT

This exercise is about expanding what you allow yourself to consider as a possibility. It's about creating space between the static *no* and the dynamic *yes*.

Create two columns on a piece of paper. In the left column, write "The Story I'm Telling Myself," and in the right column, "What Else Could Be True?"

Under "The Story I'm Telling Myself," write down the limiting narratives you've caught yourself repeating. Be specific. Write what you actually think.

Examples:

- I'm too old to switch careers at this point.
- I don't have the right background for leadership roles.
- I can't start a business.
- I'm not entrepreneurial.
- That opportunity is for someone more qualified/ experienced/connected than me.

In the right column, ask yourself: What's another way to look at this? What evidence contradicts my story?

Examples:

- **I'm too old to switch careers now becomes:** People switch careers at every age. My experience is an asset, not a disadvantage. I have clarity about what I want that I didn't have at twenty-five.
- **I don't have the right background for leadership roles becomes:** Leadership is learned, not inherited. I've led projects and people for over five years. I can develop the specific skills I'm missing.
- **I can't start a business, I'm not entrepreneurial becomes:** I don't know yet if I'm entrepreneurial because I haven't tried. I have skills that businesses need. I could start small and test it.
- **That opportunity is for someone more qualified than me becomes:** I'm going to let them decide if I'm qualified. They expressed an interest in speaking to me.

After you've completed both columns, read what you wrote in "What Else Could Be True?" This isn't a one-time exercise; it's an activity you can return to whenever you notice your inner chatter. You're training your brain to pause before defaulting to a static reflex.

One client keeps this exercise on her phone and pulls it up whenever she's about to decline an opportunity out of fear. She says it's become her *possibility policy.*

Shifting from a static to a dynamic mindset isn't an overnight activity. Here are some words and actions that make all the difference:

The power of *yet*. This tiny word changes everything. "I can't do that" becomes "I can't do that yet." "I don't know how" becomes "I don't know how yet." *Yet* implies that change is possible, that you're on a journey, that your current state isn't your permanent state.

Positive reframe. Carol Dweck's research shows that people with a growth mindset view setbacks as information, not personal failure. They ask "What did I learn?" rather than "What's wrong with me?" This creates positively skewed insights.

Building evidence. Your brain believes what you tell it, especially on repeat. If you've been telling it "I'm not capable" for years, that's the story you carry. You have to build counter evidence. Keep a running list of:

- Times you learned something new that felt hard at first
- Challenges you overcame that you didn't think you could
- Skills you have now that you once didn't have
- Positive feedback others have given you that contradicts your limiting beliefs

When the static mindset whispers "You can't," you pull out your evidence list to remind you that you, indeed, can.

Remember: Your brain defaults to negativity because it's trying to keep you safe, but safe isn't the same as fulfilled.

The thing that feels riskiest, reaching for what you actually want, is often less risky than staying stuck in work that drains you. You do not need to overhaul your entire mindset overnight, nor can you. However, you can start with these practices:

Start before you're ready. Confidence comes from action, not the other way around. Bina discovered this when she finally asked for a conversation to discuss a promotion. The fear didn't go away first, but she moved forward anyway, and the confidence came after.

Keeping a journal of her thoughts also helped her think more intentionally about her future aspirations because she was in a better headspace. She was, in a sense, talking to herself more kindly, using empowering language, and that increased her self-esteem. She was feeling much better about herself all around.

A few months later, she had the opportunity to interview for a more senior role in-house. We had practiced mock interviews so when the time came, she was ready. And you know what? She got the promotion.

ACTIVITY: MAINTAINING YOUR MINDSET MUSCLE

Mindset work isn't a one-and-done. It's not like you do the Possibility Pivot activity once and you're cured of negative thinking. Creating new neural pathways takes repetition.

Think of it like building muscle. You don't go to the gym once and become strong that same week. You show up consistently, you practice your exercises, and over time, you find yourself lifting more weight with ease. The same is true for your mindset muscle.

Here are a couple of reflections to explore at your mindset gym:

What If I Believed I Could Figure This Out?

- Capture one piece of evidence. What happened today that proves you're more capable than your static mindset gives you credit for? Write it down. Build your evidence file.
- Review your language. Look back at emails, texts, journal entries. How much static versus dynamic language do you use?
- What opportunity did you dismiss this week without fully considering it? What made you dismiss it? Was that a realistic assessment or your static mindset?
- The goal isn't to eliminate doubt or fear. The goal is to stop letting doubt and fear make all your decisions. You can feel scared and still move forward. You can doubt yourself and still try.

When You're Stuck in Place: Navigating Your Runway

You've audited your ecosystem, you know what's not working, and you're ready for something different. But you can't leave yet, or make a change—maybe for financial reasons, maybe you're supporting your family, or the timing just isn't right.

If this is where you are at the moment, please know this is normal and one of the hardest phases. There's a space between deciding you want a shift and that shift actually occurring. I call it your runway. Once you make the decision, you expect to take off quickly—whether it's for a new role, new energy, fresh circumstances. But it rarely happens that fast. Instead, you find yourself taxiing on the runway, for months or even years, watching others take off while you're still waiting for clearance. It's deeply frustrating.

This is when your mindset becomes your most important tool.

What to Do While You Wait

While you are taxiing on the runway, you can use this time with intention. If you can't change your circumstances as quickly as you would like, you can use this time to learn from this moment:

- What am I learning that will serve me later?
- What skills am I building in this situation?
- What do I now know I want—or don't want—in my next role?

This is a time for you to get perspective and extract insights from this moment.

Revisiting Values

We talked about values in chapter 5. If you can't honor all your values at work right now, look for places where you can honor them. If you value creativity but your role is rigid, join an artistic group. Your values don't have to be satisfied only at work.

It is about staying engaged while you build toward what's next. Even when you're counting down hours, dreading Monday mornings, feeling like this will never end—it will pass. It always does. Nothing lasts forever. I know it may not feel that way at the moment, but shifts occur and movement follows. You are already on your runway, gathering speed for takeoff.

Key Points:

- **Your Dynamic Mindset Determines Your Destination.** A static mindset filters out possibilities before they can become real options. A dynamic mindset expands opportunities and possibilities.
- **Fear Falsely Protects You.** The four most common fears—visibility, being "found out," imperfection, and disappointing others—create barriers that feel like safety but keep you stuck and prevent you from reaching for fulfilling work.
- ***Yet* is a Portal.** Adding *yet* to "I can't" or "I don't know how" transforms limitation into possibility and reminds you that your current state isn't permanent and that you will work through it.
- **Words Need a Workout.** Like building muscle, shifting from static to dynamic thinking takes repetition. Regular reflection, tracking your language

patterns, and building evidence of your abilities strengthens your mindset over time.

- **The Runway Prepares You for Takeoff.** The period between decision and action is rarely quick, but it serves a purpose—gaining clarity and staying attuned to what captures your attention.

PART IV

VISION: WHERE DO YOU SEE YOURSELF?

Designing your future with intention and clarity

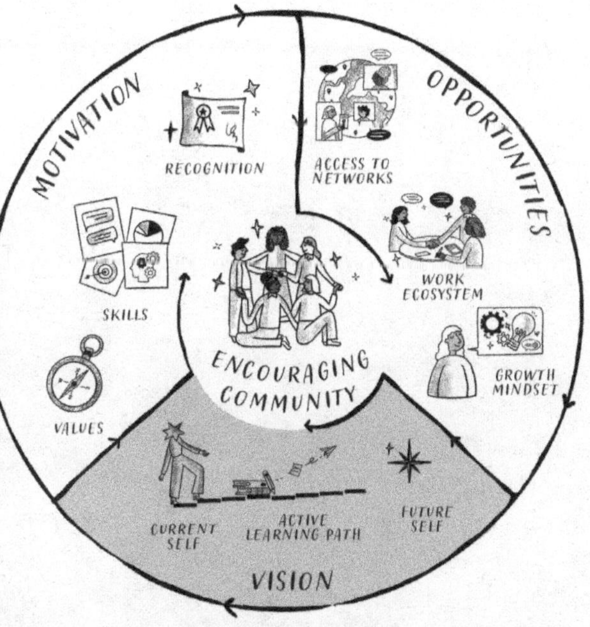

THE MOVE FRAMEWORK©

CHAPTER 12

PERSONAL VISION

What do you want?

Although this sounds like a simple enough question, chances are you aren't able to answer it easily. Your response shouldn't be about what looks good on paper, nor what others want for you. It's about what you desire: your personal vision.

Your personal vision is an image of your future, a portrait of who you're becoming or who you wish to become. It's the answer to, "If you were living your best life, what would it look like?" And like your identity, it's not static.

Vision is a magnet that pulls you to your desired self. It's your portal to permission, to dream big. In a world that often tries to keep women small and selfless or where women keep their dreams to themselves, exploring personal vision requires you to claim your ambitions with courage. Yet most of us seldom let ourselves do so.

So, what is it that you truly want?

I ask because you likely have an aspiration, something that tickles at your heart and mind. Whether it's a wish to learn a new language or to set up your own business, or even the desire to spend more time with your family, there's always a pull toward something. It can be a teeny-tiny thought or a whisper morphing into a wail, but it's there.

Your vision from just a few years ago likely doesn't fit who you are today. Career development research shows we move through natural transitions—new roles, shifting priorities, evolving values—that call for periodic recalibration of what fulfillment means now. This recalibration isn't optional—it's essential. Studies reveal that women who develop a personal vision experience greater self-efficacy, fulfillment, and more genuine engagement in their work. A clear vision honors your values and aspirations.

In the next three chapters, we will unpack the journey to identifying your personal vision, the path to who you're becoming. First, we'll review your current self, or who you are right now, including the values, skills, and experiences that have shaped you so far. Then, we'll explore your future self: who you're becoming in your quest for more fulfillment. Lastly, we will explore your Active Learning Path: the road map that will help you to close your fulfillment gap.

Let's begin by taking stock of where you stand today.

CHAPTER 13

CURRENT SELF: WHO AM I?

In chapter 12, you were introduced to the concept of personal vision, but before you can envision your future self you need to understand your current self. Women who find themselves stuck in their work life often tell me they feel like they're standing at a crossroads without a map. They want something to change, but they can't articulate what. This is because they're trying to plan their future without fully understanding their present.

Emilie had voiced that exact concern. She put down her pencil on my dining room table and let out a huge sigh. The drawing I asked her to scribble looked like a rollercoaster. We were at my apartment, and I had brought out a flip chart and a box of crayons. Murmuring in the background was my instrumental jazz playlist courtesy of Spotify.

Emilie had just completed the lifeline activity, one of my favorite exploratory exercises when it comes to taking stock of one's experiences. But before I tell you what Emilie discovered in that drawing, let me explain why this exercise matters so much on the journey toward fulfillment.

In Part II (Chapters 4–7), we explored the importance of motivation and the various components that make it up: namely our values, skills, and recognition, all of which are already part of who you are at your essence. You have already begun the work of understanding your current self. What we don't often see is the full picture of what has contributed to who we are today. We are quick to focus on moments in our lives that feel consequential but gloss over the arc of our larger story.

But how do we see the full picture? How do we move from understanding the individual values and skills that make up motivation to recognizing the patterns that define us? This is where storytelling becomes a strategic career tool. By mapping your life as a narrative, you can identify the throughlines, those red threads that are the connective tissue of your experiences, and reveal who you are today.

Psychologist Dan McAdams's work on narrative identity shows that the stories we tell about ourselves aren't just reflections of who we are. They shape our identity and future choices. His work illustrates that people who can articulate a story that connects their past experiences to their present self and future aspirations report higher levels of well-being.

As Danish philosopher Søren Kierkegaard wrote, "Life can only be understood backwards but must be lived forwards." Who you are today is the starting point for an exploration of who you are wanting to become.

I know this intimately because of my own upbringing. I was born in London to Jamaican and Guyanese parents, raised in Switzerland, and have worked and lived in a number of countries. My multicultural background has been both a strength and a challenge, teaching me to bridge worlds while sometimes making me feel I don't fully belong to a particular one. Your identities not only shape how you see yourself but how the world responds to you. I chose New York for the multiculturalism that thrives there, where I feel right at home doing the work I love, championing people's careers. It would be misguided to think that my origin story doesn't impact who I wanted to become. And the same is true for you. All of us are influenced by where our lives began. And because of that, our starting point is deeply embedded in where we end up.

EMILIE'S STORY

When we first met at my career workshop, Emilie introduced herself as the deputy director of a health services division in a small humanitarian organization. She had spent close to two decades in the field, running programs across three continents. Her bio was impressive and she was certainly proud of all that she had accomplished. But lately she'd felt like she was teetering on a tightrope, caught between family commitments and her work obligations. She wasn't complaining as both were what she had always wanted, but she felt she was stretched beyond what she could handle. And she also knew that people looked to her as a model worker, spouse, parent, and colleague. She was overwhelmed and yet she felt like she ought to be grateful for the position she now had.

But when she asked herself what her larger aspiration was, she was concerned that she didn't seem to know. In her late forties, she wanted to both enjoy her full-time job and feel fulfilled by her life. And yet something was missing that she couldn't quite place her finger on.

"I love the work I do," she told me in one of our early sessions. "But I'm not sure the job is good for me anymore. It's too much, and I can't seem to have enough energy to sustain this pace. I also don't want to let anyone down as this is the dream setup and I should be over the moon."

What do you hear when you read Emilie's story? Have you ever found yourself thinking the same thing? You get to the top of the mountain that you thought you wanted to climb, only to realize that not only are you exhausted but the view is cloudy and there's not much to take in after all. You've perhaps been climbing for someone else, or you've climbed because you thought it was expected of you. The thing we thought we wanted has turned out to be disappointing and disorienting.

Psychologist E. Tory Higgins distinguishes between our current self, our ideal (or, in this case, future) self, and our *ought* self, the person we think we should be based on others' expectations of us. The ought self can oftentimes overshadow who you are and who you are becoming, and the challenge is reconnecting to your essence. Emilie's ought self was center stage.

Emilie needed the opportunity to take stock of where she'd been and where she was headed, so I offered her the Draw Your Lifeline activity you'll do at the end of this chapter to visually map out her personal and professional trajectory. When I gave her the assignment I asked her to pay close attention to uplifting experiences, challenges, and turning points. In doing so, my hope was that she could identify patterns and themes that have shaped who she is today.

EMILIE'S LIFELINE

Emilie's lifeline activity was more than a timeline, it was a blueprint of her life. The line she drew had sharp peaks and deep valleys and areas that looked like crevasses. The peaks were moments of deep connection: launching a new program in East Africa, the birth of her children, and being promoted to manager soon after her postgraduate degree. The valleys were transitions: relocating for her partner's job, losing a mentor to cancer, the restructuring of an organization she had been deeply attached to that had resulted in an overhaul of the management team.

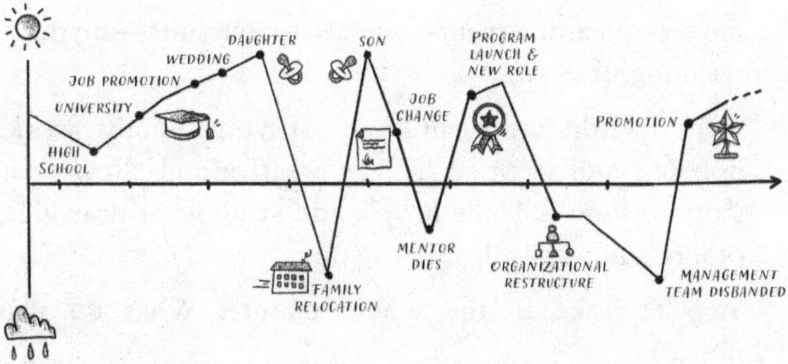

Now it's your turn.

ACTIVITY: DRAW YOUR LIFELINE

You'll need: a large sheet of paper (a flip chart works well), colored pencils, and a good thirty minutes of uninterrupted time.

Step 1: Draw a horizontal line across your page representing your life from your earliest memory to today.

Step 2: Mark significant events, both positive and negative, above and below the line. Place events above the line that were moments of joy, peak experiences, those times when things went well. Place moments of sorrow, tough moments, and times when things worked against you below the line.

Step 3: The height above or depth below the line represents the emotional intensity of the experience.

Step 4: Include professional achievements, family milestones, educational experiences, relationships, losses, moves, health events, creative pursuits—anything meaningful to you.

Step 5: Add representations of your family, work, hobbies, and spiritual life. Be creative and allow your story to unfold. Some people add symbols or drawings, others add words. It's up to you.

Step 6: Take in the whole picture. What do you notice?

Reflective Questions

Once you've completed your lifeline, take time to answer these questions thoughtfully, at your own pace.

PART 1: Pattern Recognition

- What do my high points have in common?
- What do my low points have in common?
- What common threads run through my lifeline?

PART 2: Values Identification

- Looking at peak moments, what values were being honored?
- When did I feel most authentically myself?
- In what situations are my values compromised. What did I learn from that?

PART 3: Skills Recognition

- What activities was I doing during my peak moments?
- What activities show up in the valleys?
- What types of experiences bring me satisfaction?

PART 4: Recognition Patterns

- When have I felt most seen and valued?
- What was I being recognized for in those moments?
- What is the gap, if any, between what I'm recognized for and what fulfills me?

PART 5: Future Insights

- What can I learn from my past experiences that informs the change I'm seeking?
- What patterns do I want to continue?
- What patterns am I ready to release?

UNDERSTANDING YOUR LIFELINE: AGENCY VERSUS CIRCUMSTANCE

Did you notice that experiences above the line are often things that you make happen versus those elements below the line are things that happen to you? This distinction between choice and circumstance can be insightful and show you how you're creating a fulfilling life. Circumstances are things you cannot avoid, such as the loss of a job, an accident, or events outside of your control. But the learning comes from what happens above the line, the choices you made to overcome your circumstances. What happens above the line can be viewed as agency: your ability to make choices and take action that shapes your life (the difference between feeling like life happens to you versus feeling like you're actively creating your life). Research on human agency, your capacity to act and influence your own life, shows that this sense of control is crucial to well-being. Psychologist Albert Bandura, who pioneered the study of agency, found that people who believe they can shape their circumstances (what he called "self-efficacy") experience greater motivation, resilience, and life satisfaction. The dips are inevitable, but what you learn from the climb is what builds your resilience along the way. Psychologist Ann Masten's research on resilience reveals that bouncing back from adversity comes from what she calls "ordinary magic," the everyday capabilities we build through facing life's challenges.

Your choices—to lean into your strengths and to do what you love—are the cornerstone of your well-being. In fact, psychologist Martin Seligman, who has studied "learned optimism," found that people who choose to focus on the bright side and view setbacks as temporary recover more quickly and experience higher levels of fulfillment. How does that inform who you are today? This exercise is a conversation with yourself. You might see something today that takes on new meaning next week—or next month. If you're finding it hard to see your own patterns, consider sharing your lifeline with someone you trust, be it a friend or a colleague. We often can't see ourselves as clearly as others can see us, and a fresh perspective can illuminate what you've been too close to notice. The goal is to start asking better questions about who you are today.

EMILIE'S DISCOVERY

When Emilie completed her lifeline and reflected on the questions, she observed a number of patterns that struck her. She saw that her peak moments weren't always about professional achievement. Yes, launching that East Africa program was there. But so was the summer she spent volunteering at a refugee camp during graduate school and the time she organized an informal mentoring circle for young women entering the humanitarian field.

"I thought my fulfillment came from running things, from being in charge," she shared, "but actually, I'm at my best when I'm in service to others. When I'm creating space for other people to grow. My title has given me a platform and resources, but it's also pulled me away from what actually makes me happy."

This is the power of the lifeline exercise. It doesn't just record events; it reveals values in action. Three main values emerged clearly from Emilie's lifeline: connection, contribution, and courage. Connection showed up in her peak moments, building teams, forming deep partnerships, creating community. Contribution appeared in her drive to do meaningful work in the humanitarian space, and courage was present in all of her work transitions.

Emilie was also struck by the valleys in her lifeline: the difficult transitions that involved ruptures in relationships, the time she had to change schools as a teenager, and when a reorganization at work dissolved a team she'd carefully built.

"I always thought I was just bad at change," she said, "but it's losing connection that is hard for me because it's something I value greatly."

Emilie came to realize that she didn't need to leave her organization. However, she needed to reshape her role. She scheduled a conversation with her supervisor and led with where she was hoping to expand her skills while also providing value to the organization. She saw that her greatest impact came from developing others, that she was energized by creating systems and spaces for people to grow, and that her deepest satisfaction came from contribution through connection. Her supervisor agreed to a six-month trial run of having her reduce her operational oversight and work on other aspects of her job she loved. It wasn't a promotion but a redesign of her role that allowed her to integrate more of what she enjoyed.

MINING YOUR LIFELINE FOR VALUES

Values, as we saw in chapter 5, are influenced by your community, culture, family and more. They are your compass and a source of data. Now you can cross-reference: Do the values that emerged from your lifeline match those you identified in chapter 5? If there's a disconnect, what does that tell you? A values gap is worth exploring. What happens if you realize that what you wanted isn't actually represented in your values? Sometimes what you think you want is actually a projection of what someone else wants for you, or something you thought you wanted. Doing this exercise brings into focus what you truly want for yourself.

When you draw your lifeline, you might notice that some of your valleys weren't just personal challenges, they were moments when you faced barriers or bias. Closing your fulfillment gap also means understanding the context in which you thrive.

Another important distinction that emerges from this work is the awareness of the difference between your identity and your role. Your role is what you do. Your identity is who you are. A company owns your role; you own you. This matters because so many women at mid-career experience role fatigue or what Stefanie Sword-Williams, whom I mentioned in Chapter 7, calls the career comedown: when you feel dissatisfaction, boredom, or burnout, even after achieving professional success. Her definition is "when you invest significant time and energy in your career, only to realize it doesn't align with your values, lifestyle or present ambitions." What was once working just isn't anymore. The role that once fit perfectly now feels constraining. But because we've conflated our role with our identity, letting go of the role feels like losing ourselves.

The lifeline exercise helps you see that you're not your job title. You're the person who has moved through all these experiences, who has maintained certain values across contexts, who has developed skills across different terrains. Your current self is who you bring to the next chapter you are writing.

" **Your current self is who you bring to the next chapter you are writing.**

WHAT NOW?

You've drawn your lifeline, identified patterns, and reviewed your values, skills, and recognition. You now have a clearer picture of who you are. Take time to sit with it. Understanding your current self isn't about judging whether you're in the right place or making the right choices. It's about creating a foundation from which you can imagine your future self, which is exactly where you're going next. In chapter 14, you'll look at how your past experiences prepare you for future possibilities.

Like a compass, it's important that you have a known point to set a direction. And that known point is you. You can't know where you're going if you don't know where you are. All roads may lead to Rome, but where and who are you today? Your identity has been forged by countless experiences. Having clarity around how those experiences have shaped you will help you to navigate the road ahead.

Key Points:

- **The Jewels of Your Journey:** The key moments that have shaped your identity, decisions, and growth trajectory can shine a light on the path forward and help identify patterns that reveal where you are at the current moment. Follow the sparkle.
- **Your Past Plays a Part:** Understanding where you've been and what you've valued along the way creates the foundation for imagining where you're going. You can't close your fulfillment gap without first understanding where you've come from.
- **Patterns Reveal Possibility:** Examine the narrative you tell yourself to recognize recurring patterns and breakthrough moments. The patterns you repeat teach you something.
- **Your Story Is Your Strategy:** The story you construct and how you make meaning of your life shapes your ability to imagine new possibilities. When you understand your narrative, you can write the next chapter with intention.
- **You Are Not Your Job Title:** Your skills, values, and way of being are part of you, independent of your job title. Building a strong sense of who you are separate from your roles creates resilience.

CHAPTER 14

BECOMING YOU: YOUR FUTURE SELF

In chapter 13, you explored your current self through the lifeline exercise, identifying the values, skills, and patterns that have shaped who you are today. That understanding is your foundation to envision the future self you are becoming.

Vision is the key to your future self. It breaks through all the *shoulds* to steer you to what's next. Yet most of us leave our future selves on the back burner because we're barely getting by in our daily lives.

Vision is a sharp tool, and yet we seldom use it except in companies with laminated vision statements plastered in boardrooms and hallways. Peter Senge, MIT professor and author of *The Fifth Discipline,* noted that organizations tend to focus on organizational vision, sidestepping personal vision in favor of the collective. But your personal vision, or what you're working toward, matters just as much. In fact, I've found that vision is the distinguishing factor between women who stay stuck and women who create the fulfilling futures they desire.

Athletes like Gabby Thomas and Coco Gauff, for example, demonstrate how envisioning your future self can successfully bring it to life. Ahead of the 2024 Paris Olympics, Thomas shared that she wrote affirmations such as "I am an Olympic champion" and visualized herself crossing the finish line first, a practice she said strengthened her confidence and helped her step into that identity before she ever became the 200-meter world champion. Tennis champion Gauff, who was inspired by Thomas, took a similar approach, writing "I will win the French Open 2025" and putting it in places where she would see those words daily. She indeed won the women's singles that year.

This isn't bragging. It's brain science. When you spend time imagining what's possible for your future, you activate the parts of your brain responsible for planning and motivation. Dr. Boyatzis's research on the ideal self shows that when we envision who we want to become, our brains light up with possibility. This triggers the Positive Emotional Attractor, or PEA, a neurological state that makes us open to learning and creativity and energized about the future.

When you focus on possibilities and what energizes you, your brain enters what researchers call the Positive Emotional Attractor—a state where you're more creative, open to new ideas, and motivated to move forward. Think of it as your brain's "green light" mode for change.

Visualization is powerful because your brain processes imagined experiences similarly to real ones. When you picture yourself in your desired future, you're building neural pathways that are the same as the ones you'll use when you actually live that future. This is called neuroplasticity: your brain's ability to create new connections based on repeated mental rehearsal. You're not just daydreaming. You're training your brain for the future you want to create.

Interestingly, the neuroscience behind personal vision reveals that our brains process our future selves as strangers. UCLA psychologist Hal Hershfield's research shows that when you imagine yourself in the future, your neural patterns look similar to thinking about someone you don't know. This explains why envisioning the future can feel so challenging. When you continually craft pictures of your possible future selves, your brain begins to recognize them as you.

Herminia Ibarra, whom I mentioned in chapter 9, suggests that you can and should explore multiple versions of your future self because a large part of the journey to becoming you is about experimentation. Having one specific image can lead to frustration while being willing to explore multiple future selves can be liberating and helpful in the brainstorming phase. The visioning exercises in this chapter aren't just imagination exercises, they're brainstorming tools for connecting your current self to your future selves. Whether you have a specific image of your future self or multiple iterations, they help you identify a stake in the ground that points you in the direction you need to be heading. This stake, your anchor, is your aspiration come to life.

Here are some ways to create an anchor:

Vision board: Collect images, words, or symbols that represent your future self. This could be a physical collage or a digital board.

Draw or sketch: Even if you're not an artist, sketching your future life—your workspace, your home, your ideal day—engages different parts of your brain.

Collect physical objects: A stone from a place you want to live, an object representing your future work, a photo capturing the feeling you're aiming for.

Voice memo: Record yourself describing your future self. Hearing your own voice articulating the vision makes it feel more real.

Your vision of your future self needs to live outside your head. Coco Gauff and Gabby Thomas wrote them out. Your future self can't stay locked in a single exercise or tucked in a journal. It needs to be externalized, written, recorded, visualized, in a way that keeps the image present and alive for you.

Your vision should be a living document, something you revisit, refine, and reconnect with regularly. When I planned on relocating to New York, my iPhone screensaver was the Empire State Building. Even locked, the visual was right there, at my fingertips: a quiet and constant reminder of what I was aiming for. Find a rhythm that keeps your vision alive without making it feel like another obligation on your to-do list. Your future self gives you decision-making criteria; when faced with a choice, you can ask, "Does this move me closer to my future self?" If your vision feels flat, obligatory, or like it belongs to someone else, that's valuable information.

GIVING YOURSELF PERMISSION TO VISION

Even when you have a vision for your future, fear and practical concerns often hold you back. You know what you want, but the obstacles feel insurmountable. Here are two examples of roadblocks that come up in creating personal visions:

Simone: "I'm golden-handcuffed to my recruiting job. I make a pretty significant amount of money. But I really want to exit it, at least in a full-time capacity, so I can focus on what I'm passionate about. I'm successful and driven, but I'm also scared to death. I grew up with a scarcity-mindset family, and so even though I've never in my life actually experienced scarcity, that doesn't prevent that scarcity mindset from entering."

Nya: "I'm a perfectionist. I like to think it through, figure it out, do my research, do my reading, get an additional degree, of which I have four right now, before I do the next thing. And that's completely insane. Branching out into a territory that I'm basically trying to vision and create for myself is scary."

If you see yourself in Simone or Nya's story, you're not alone. These obstacles—financial constraints, perfectionism, fear of disappointing others, or anything else—shouldn't stop you from imagining your future self. The difference between women who stay stuck and women who move forward isn't the absence of these fears. It's the willingness to envision their future selves despite these constraints.

Creating a dream board for your future self isn't about creating a slightly improved version of who you are today. It's about articulating and imagining a future that might feel overconfident and out of reach right now. But your future self doesn't have to follow a predictable trajectory. It's your space to dream it as you wish.

Inevitably, as we move toward who we aspire to be, limiting beliefs will surface almost immediately. As psychologist Gay Hendricks mentions in his book *The Big Leap,* fear has a hold on you that cannot be underestimated.

You might hear yourself thinking:

"I'm too old to start something new."

"This isn't practical."

"I should be grateful for what I have."

"My family needs me to stay on this path."

When that voice rises up, ask yourself: whose voice are you actually hearing?

Maya, a primary-school teacher who wanted to move to working for a nonprofit, told herself she was too old to start something new at forty-seven. But when I asked her who told her that, she said, "my mother." Once Maya identified that her mother believed she had to choose her career by age thirty and stick with it, she could start reframing it to, "What if age is actually an advantage?" and: "What if I have wisdom and experience that a younger version of me didn't have?" That reframe opened up space for her to rewrite the narrative of her life.

These voices are not your vision; don't let them take the pen. You can acknowledge them and remind yourself that you're just exploring your vision. You're not handcuffing yourself to a specific future. Don't your current fears try to keep you safe. When the limiting beliefs arise, acknowledge them, then ask: What would my future self say to this fear? What statement do I most often make about why I can't pursue what I want? Whose voice is speaking the loudest: mine, my family, my culture, my friends?

> **When the limiting beliefs arise, acknowledge them, then ask: What would my future self say to this fear? What statement do I most often make about why I can't pursue what I want? Whose voice is speaking the loudest: mine, my family, my culture, my friends?**

RELATIONSHIPS AND YOUR FUTURE SELF

One question I hear often: How much should my vision of my future self take into account my relationships, be it partner, children, aging parents? It's a fair question, especially for women who've spent years putting others' needs first. Your future self can and should include relationships, but it needs to be your vision of what those relationships look like, not only serving others. The women who thrive don't choose between family and self. They reimagine what both could look like in their future. When my former colleague Rachel first envisioned her future self, she felt somewhat guilty listing professional ambitions because her children were young. We talked through ways she could reframe her vision, and something she came up with was, "What if my future self models for my daughters what it looks like to pursue meaningful work?" Your future self doesn't exist in isolation, but you shouldn't disappear into everyone else's futures either.

ACTIVITY: A DAY IN THE LIFE OF YOUR FUTURE SELF

Write a detailed narrative of a single day in your future life.

How it works:

Find a quiet space and set aside thirty minutes. You have the option to do the following activity in one of two ways.

Option 1: Pen and paper. Close your eyes. Imagine you've fast forwarded ten to fifteen years into the future. You are your future self now, the person you've wanted to become. You're living the life you've envisioned. Walk through a regular day in your life. Not a special occasion, but an ordinary Tuesday. What does a fulfilling day look like for your future self?

As you write, here are some prompts to help you envision:

- Where are you? What do you see when you open your eyes?
- What does your morning routine look like?
- How do you spend your time?
- What are you experiencing?
- Who are the people around you?
- How do you feel throughout the day? What emotions are present?
- What do you do in the evening? How does the day close?
- What makes this day feel fulfilling?

Keep these notes close by and refer to them regularly. You can also send this as an electronic letter to your future self (for free) via futureme.org to be delivered via email to you on a date of your choosing.

Option 2: Voice record. A way to deepen your connection with your future self is to record your questions and answers. Research has found that hearing your voice can strengthen your attachment to your future self, making it feel more real. Ask yourself the same questions but this time, hit record as you ideate about your future self's day.

Once you've walked through your day as your future self, take the time to capture what you discovered, in writing or through a voice note:

- What surprised you most about your future self?
- What did you expect to matter that didn't?

- How does your future self feel different from who you are today?
- What qualities does your future self have that your current self is developing?
- What's already present in your current life that connects to your future self?
- What's completely missing from your current life that your future self has embraced?
- What elements of this day felt most essential, the non-negotiables of your future?

The answers that are being surfaced will serve as stepping stones to who you are becoming, and these details matter as they'll guide your learning path in chapter 15.

What to Do If You're Stuck

Sometimes when you sit down to envision your future self, it's just a blank slate. I have seen it happen on a number of occasions.

If that happens, here's what you can do:

Start with what you don't want. Sometimes it's easier to identify what you're moving away from rather than what you're moving towards. List all the things you don't want: a long commute to work, company politics, living far from family, working eighty-plus hours a week. Then flip the script, and write down the opposite. This gives you a starting point to what you desire.

Revisit moments of joy. Recall moments in the past year when you felt energized, engaged, fully yourself. What were you doing? Who were you with? What about that experience made it feel good? This will help remind yourself of your moments of joy.

Borrow from others. Think about people whose lives you admire. What is it about their work, their schedule, their lifestyle that appeals to you? This gives you clues as to what matters to you.

Explore your envy. Author and podcaster Mel Robbins talks about envy being a guide. She refers to envy as blocked desire. What are you envious of? Your answer is pointing you in the direction of what you would like for yourself. Use it as your informant.

Go big. Ask yourself: what would you do if you weren't afraid? What would you pursue if you knew you couldn't fail? This will help you separate your future self from fear-based limitations.

Look back. Imagine your future self looking back at you now. What would your future self say to your current self? What would she thank you for? What would she wish you had started sooner?

The key is to keep the questions open and to stay curious. What you want your life to look like should be at the forefront of your mind. Pay attention to what captures your attention, what you spend your money on, and what you find yourself drawn to on social media, even. These are clues.

You might create a vision and then find that weeks or months later, you're pulled toward something different. This is normal and often happens because we're stimulated by so many external factors and new ideas arise all the time. Your vision can evolve as you grow and learn more about yourself. The exercise isn't meant to lock you into one path forever; it's meant to give you a clear enough direction to start moving one step at a time. Trust that as you take action and identify a learning path, your future self will come into sharper focus.

Key Points:

- **Vision Is Not the Same as Goals:** Goals activate stress and narrow focus. Vision activates hope and expands possibility. You need both, but vision comes first.
- **Your Brain Doesn't Distinguish Between Imagined and Real:** Vivid visualization creates neural pathways that support your future reality.
- **Talking About Your Vision Amplifies It:** Share your vision with people who can hold space for possibility.
- **Vision Is a Living Document:** Your vision will evolve as you grow. Revisit it quarterly. Refine it. Let it change with you.
- **Your Future Is Here.** Your future self is already forming. The choices you make today are helping you create the future you want for yourself. Be intentional about what you want.

CHAPTER 15

YOUR ACTIVE LEARNING PATH

Everything you've explored so far in this book has led you here. Your values, skills, sources of recognition, networks, work ecosystem, mindset, and vision are no longer abstract concepts. Together, they form a blueprint for what comes next, ensuring that what you've learned continues to shape how you live and work today and beyond.

As you'll see, this chapter is about staying in motion. The Active Learning Path we will dig into will help you translate insight into sustained action. It's not about doing more but rather about designing movement that keeps you learning, adjusting, and closing your fulfillment gap over time. I call this *movementum.* Movement underpinned by momentum.

> "I call this *movementum:* movement underpinned by momentum."

Movement itself changes your brain. Dr. John Ratey's research in *Spark: The Revolutionary New Science of Exercise and the Brain* shows that physical activity enhances cognitive function, emotional regulation, and learning by increasing neurochemicals associated with motivation and focus. When you're in motion, you're not just taking action toward your aspirations, you're also creating internal conditions that make change easier to sustain. You'll also learn additional ways of sustaining movementum, like rituals, habits, experimentation, and accountability.

Your Active Learning Path is a roadmap, not just another exercise to complete. It's your *how* in motion. How you will get from A to B. How you will go from your current setup to what you are yearning for. So far, we've explored motivation to reveal your *why.* Opportunities showed you the *where.* Vision clarified the *what* and the Active Learning Path sets up the *how.* It's the journey that supports your vision from possibility into reality.

That journey can feel daunting at times, as though you're moving carefully in the dark. There's a term for this period of time: liminality, that space between what's known and unknown. This in-between space can feel unsettling, but it's also where learning takes place.

Research consistently shows that intention alone is rarely enough. Across studies of behavior change, 60 to 70 percent fail to translate into sustained action. The gap is rarely motivation. It's structure. The Active Learning Path provides that structure where learning continues even when motivation drags.

Without a plan, you risk what I call "post-session slump," when you emerge from a workshop buzzing with energy only to wilt a week later because you've lost the scaffolding that held you up. Let's avoid that slump by putting a plan in place. Not something that's static but rather a series of dynamic guideposts that you can come back to again and again.

Remember, all of the activities you've done so far in this book are now in your backpack. Your completed exercises, notes, and reflections can become touchstones on your journey, ready to guide you whenever you need them. You'll draw on all of the activities as you design your Active Learning Path later in this chapter. Take a moment to look back at what you've explored so far:

- Values and what matters most to you
- Skills and where you feel energized
- Experiences of recognition and contribution
- Networks and relationships
- Work ecosystem
- Growth mindset
- Current self and emerging future self

Now you have everything ready for the journey ahead!

RITUALS, HABITS, EXPERIMENTS, AND ACCOUNTABILITY

Your Active Learning Path isn't about perfection, it's about progress. As I mentioned earlier in this chapter, there are four reliable ways to sustain movementum: rituals, habits, experimentation, and accountability. You don't need all four at once. Even one is enough to begin. Each serves a distinct role in closing your fulfillment gap.

RITUALS

According to neuroscientist Anne-Laure Le Cunff, author of *Tiny Experiments,* rituals are "intentional practices that carry meaning." They help you mark transitions, maintain momentum, and connect to something larger than yourself. Your brain benefits from rituals because about 40 percent of your daily actions are driven by unconscious patterns. Rituals interrupt those autopilot activities and create intentional moments where you reconnect with your vision and values. They're the scaffolding that supports your active learning.

> Georgia O'Keeffe took a daily thirty-minute desert walk before painting. Leonard Cohen developed a pre-performance ritual of chanting a Latin song with his band before going onstage. Rituals focus on why you're doing something, they're your internal chatter interrupter, forcing you to pause and open space for contemplation. They are micro moments of joy.

I think of rituals as being represented in three different formats:

- **Visual rituals** mark significant moments. I mentioned in chapter 14 that part of my journey of relocating to New York was to make my iPhone screensaver the Empire State Building. Even when my phone was locked, that image was a constant reminder of my ambition. What visual ritual could support your journey?
- **Movementum rituals** are regular check-ins with yourself that keep you learning and adjusting. Perhaps it's a weekly Sunday evening session where you review your progress and celebrate wins, or a monthly vision check-in where you revisit your future self.
- **Connection rituals** bring in other people, whether a friend, mentor, or colleague. This is an intentional gathering with a shared purpose. One of my clients meets with her accountability partner every other Thursday morning for virtual coffee. They each share one win, one challenge, and one commitment for the weeks ahead.

Rituals remind you why you're on a certain path. They're one powerful entry point, but habits, experiments, and accountability are equally effective ways to sustain movementum. Choose the one that feels most accessible right now.

HABITS

Marshall Goldsmith, author and executive coach, titled his book *What Got You Here Won't Get You There.* As you explore ways to find more contentment in life and work, whether in your current role, in a new department, in an entirely different company, or as a solopreneur, your exploration requires you to develop different habits. Habits are automatic behaviors, unconscious routines like brushing your teeth. Seth Godin, bestselling author of *Tribes: We Need You to Lead Us,* describes routines as "decisions not made," freeing up brain space for what matters. Habits make action easier while rituals make action meaningful.

EXPERIMENTS

Experiments give you permission to explore without putting pressure on yourself. When you frame actions as experiments, you collect data that offers further insights instead of judging the outcomes. The experimental mindset gives you permission to explore with curiosity. Not all experiments need to be grand initiatives. In fact, some of the most powerful learning comes from small actions that help you test ideas without cornering yourself. These might include shadowing a colleague in a different department for a few hours, attending one networking event in a field you're curious about, or volunteering for a project outside your usual scope. The joy of tiny actions is that they're easy to start, quick to learn from, and simple to adjust. They lower the barrier to exploration and make experimentation feel less daunting.

Whether your experiments are tiny or transformative, they all serve the same purpose: gathering data about what energizes you and what doesn't.

Here are some ways to experiment:

- **Be an influencer (not the social media kind):** If you're thinking about ways to have positive influence, consider creating platforms for others. One friend, frustrated with siloed thinking and craving more strategic work, proposed a quarterly "Cross-Functional Leadership Forum," bringing together senior leaders from different divisions to discuss organizational challenges and collaborative solutions. She volunteered to facilitate the first three sessions, which addressed a real business need while also helping her gain visibility across the organization, build relationships, and test whether she enjoyed convening and strategic facilitation more than her current operational role. Within a year, she had vastly increased her visibility and presence in the company and was far more content in her work life. She used her influence to reorganize a work stream that served both the organization and her own reinvention.
- **Sit on a board:** Joining a board helps you sharpen your skill set, build new networks, gain visibility, and test a sector that might energize you.
- **Pivot in place:** My former neighbor, Nicole, a fifteen-year veteran in her company's food division, assumed her restlessness meant she needed to leave her role. After four months of strategic exploration,

virtual and in-person coffee chats with the beverages team, and volunteering for cross-functional projects, she proactively proposed a six-month rotational assignment developing cross-category innovations. Her initial conversations went nowhere, her boss was hesitant, and the pilot took months to negotiate. She did eventually land in a different role that had her learn a whole new side of the industry. The company retained fifteen years of institutional knowledge and Nicole rekindled her passion without starting over. A win-win. Her lesson was that sometimes the most fulfilling move is *across* rather than *out*.

ACCOUNTABILITY

One of the most valuable aspects of movementum is accountability. When you share your intentions with someone else, your chance of following through increases dramatically. You create movement where there wasn't any before. A study found that you have a 65 percent chance of completing a goal if you tell someone you're going to do it, and if you add a specific check-in, your chance of success rises to 95 percent!

Effective accountability is like a three-legged stool. It needs three distinct parts: an accountability partner, a set of questions, and a follow-up meeting. Once you've identified your commitment and action, your accountability partner should ask you "By when will it be completed?" followed by "How will you know?"— meaning how will you know you've completed the task? These two questions hold your feet to the proverbial fire without judgment. Don't forget to commit to a follow-up date in your calendar before you end the meeting.

> Make sure your accountability partner is a person invested in your growth and in helping you cultivate joy. Someone who:
>
> - Celebrates, not dims, your wins
> - Asks curious questions rather than giving advice
> - Holds space for your learning, including what didn't work
> - Shows up consistently and keeps their commitments

This isn't necessarily your best friend or colleague (though they could be). This is someone who's a cheerleader without being attached to specific outcomes. They want you to succeed in your way, not theirs.

THE REALITY OF FINDING TIME

Throughout this book, I've mentioned finding pockets of time to complete exercises. I know for some of you, this feels like a luxurious ask. Who has any free time? The juggle struggle makes it nearly impossible to imagine more hours in the day. So, what can you do to carve out pockets of time?

Here are some suggestions:

Rise and Shine: Set your alarm twenty minutes early to read one article, drink your coffee in silence, or prepare for your day. That's one hour and forty minutes for yourself if you do it five days a week. For night owls, carve out those twenty minutes in the evening instead.

Wait and Wonder: If you're waiting for your son's hockey practice to finish, for example, rather than doomscroll, make that your voice-memo moment.

Commute Cocoon: Whether driving or on the train, listen to an audiobook or simply spend time in deep reflection. Protecting your time cocoon is one of the key factors in sustaining joy.

Lunch and Learn: Pick one day where you eat at your desk but close your email. Those twenty minutes become your mid-week check-in. What's working? What needs adjustment?

Walk and Talk: Merge two tasks: Get your steps in while reconnecting with someone you don't often have a chance to speak to.

Notice what these have in common? They help you layer intentions while on the move, turning otherwise mindless moments into purposeful ones. But eventually, you'll need to make harder choices. You can redesign moments for a while, but real change requires letting go of something to make room for what matters more. As you start making your moves, you'll need to subtract one activity and replace it with another. You may feel you have no time, but that will never change until you intentionally open up a slot. Only you can do that.

What are you willing to stop doing en route to becoming you?

MAKING YOUR WORDS WORK FOR YOU

Some people thrive working toward goals, targets to hit, and milestones to reach. Others feel constrained by the word *goals* and prefer words like *aspirations* or *intentions,* which can reduce the pressure to perform. The words you use shape how you approach your path.

Goals work for those who thrive on strategy and corporate speak, those looking for specific targets.

Intentions suggest something you're working toward in a more unattached manner while still being focused on the outcome.

Aspirations help you look to the future with less pressure, seeking out that which inspires you.

Ambitions signal serious commitment.

The destination is the same, but perhaps one of these terms feels more aligned with how you view your endeavors. Whichever works best for you is your compass.

What is your word of choice?

Let me share Margaret's story, which demonstrates how this path works in practice.

Margaret's word was *goal.* She had spent over fifteen years at a major pharmaceutical company, the last seven at the senior level overseeing a large team. On paper, she had everything: title, compensation, and peer respect, but she was exhausted in a way a vacation couldn't fix. Her aging mother needed increasing support and her youngest was finishing college. She was a single parent and she knew continuing her work in pharmaceuticals wasn't sustainable, but the thought of starting something new was paralyzing. How could she pivot into a new job or new field after spending two decades building expertise? She decided her goal would be to reduce her hours and gain flexibility while still working in the field that she loved.

Together, we designed her Active Learning Path, honoring both her constraints and her considerable strengths. An Active Learning Path is the structure that supports your journey, like lanterns on a walkway that show you the way.

We began by creating rituals together:

- Waking up thirty minutes early to journal and plan out her week.
- Every Friday, she ate lunch with her email closed and gave herself twenty minutes to review what she'd learned that week and one way she'd make an adjustment for the following week.
- A monthly coffee or meetup with a former colleague who'd successfully transitioned to consulting. They held each other accountable and shared resources.

Some experiments she tried included:

Month 1–3: Increased thought leadership on LinkedIn, writing about healthcare innovation. She started building her external brand.

Month 4–6: Joined the board of a health-advocacy nonprofit. This gave her visibility outside her company and let her test whether nonprofit work energized her. (It did.)

Month 7–9: Spoke at three industry conferences. She discovered she loved speaking and teaching.

Month 10–12: Negotiated a transition to a part-time consulting arrangement with her company, leveraging her years of relationships and expertise while freeing time for board work, speaking engagements, and caring for her mother. Her income decreased but she was more fulfilled.

In a recent coaching session together Margaret shared something that stuck with me. "I should have transitioned to a part-time consulting arrangement at my company at forty," she said. "But I wouldn't have had the credibility to negotiate this arrangement. I wouldn't have had the network or known how to go about it. The timing was right. I feel ready now."

Margaret's story demonstrates how the Active Learning Path brings together everything we've learned so far. Notice how she:

- Acted on her core values (family time, meaningful work) that she'd clarified for herself.
- Leveraged her skills strategically rather than abandoning them.
- Created opportunities for recognition in new spaces (board work, speaking).

- Shifted her work ecosystem to one that better supported her well-being.
- Built a bridge from her current to her future self through experiments that tested her vision before fully committing.

She spent time tracking insights, not just actions, asking herself: What am I learning? What's working? What needs adjustment?

LINEA'S STORY

Linea's story shows how creating an Active Learning Path can put the pieces in place for a geographic move. Linea, a recent Yale graduate, had just started working for one of the big four consulting groups in New York.

Linea dreamed of relocating from the US to France to join her fiancé. Overwhelmed by such a major life transition, she initially felt uncertain about maintaining momentum during this big move. We started with her vision—joining her partner in France within nine months—and her aspiration (the word she chose): securing a job at an international organization.

Her rituals included weekly Sunday planning sessions, daily thirty-minute French practice, and monthly reflections where she updated her visual representation: a black-and-white drawing of the Eiffel Tower that she colored in as she completed steps. Her experiments treated job applications as learning opportunities, with informational interviews helping her understand the French job market. She kept detailed spreadsheets tracking not just applications but rejections and insights from each interaction.

With biweekly coaching for accountability, Linea landed a job just shy of her nine-month deadline. She lives in Paris with her now-husband. Voilà! More importantly, she gained confidence in her ability to navigate this move and find work life joy.

PANIC AND POTHOLES ALONG THE PATH

You'll have periods of rapid growth and periods of panic. There will be disappointments, breakthroughs, plateaus, and leaps forward. The path will have potholes. You'll miss rituals, experiments will fail, you'll change your mind, your accountability partner might disappear. The list goes on. A major project at work might derail everything. Knowing this, here are some ways to swerve to avoid the potholes:

Don't start from scratch: You don't need a new plan, as the work you've done in this book doesn't expire. If you've gotten lost along the journey, you can certainly pick up where you left off. Missed two weeks of morning rituals? Start tomorrow morning. The path is still there waiting for you.

Shrink your experiments: If carving out fifteen minutes feels too hard right now, try just taking two minutes to reset. If weekly check-ins feel overwhelming, try a monthly approach. Author and scientist BJ Fogg's research on behavior design shows that shrinking the behavior, making it so small it's nearly effortless, is more effective than waiting until you have enough time. Any movementum is a win for you.

Reach and reactivate: If you're struggling to set up three elements (rituals, experiments, accountability), then just start with one. Usually, reactivating your accountability partner is the fastest way to rebuild momentum. It's as simple as sending a text: "I got off track, I would love to resume our calls."

Wake your why: Reread your vision of your future self from chapter 14 to remind you of what you want. It's my hope that at this point in the book, when you feel stuck, unclear, or overwhelmed, you now have clarity on who you are, what you want, and how to get there.

Talk to yourself kindly: How you speak to yourself matters as much as what you do. Psychologist Ethan Kross's research on "psychological distancing" reveals that talking to yourself in the third person ("Sam can do this") rather than first person ("I can do this") creates emotional distance that helps you overcome challenges and manage stress more effectively. When you use your name or "you" instead of "I," you activate the same neural circuits you'd use when giving advice to a friend, which means you're naturally kinder and more solution focused.

This psychological shift extends beyond self-talk. What you wear and how you present yourself also influences performance. In a study by researchers Rachel White and Emily Prager, children wearing Batman costumes persevered longer on challenging tasks compared to when wearing regular clothes. The children embodied the superhero's determination, a phenomenon called "enclothed cognition." Whether it's speaking to yourself in the third person or putting on clothes that make you feel capable, these small shifts align with a growth mindset giving you greater joy and satisfaction.

At this point in your journey, you've gathered an array of powerful activities for your backpack, many if not most of which you've done along the way. Now it's time to put them into action. The following activity doesn't need to be completed in one sitting. Feel free to return to it over a few days.

ACTIVITY: DESIGN YOUR MOVEMENTUM PLAN

Before you begin, one important note: This activity works even if you complete only part of it. If you answer a few questions and take one small step, you're doing it right. You can come back to the rest over a few days.

You've moved through this entire book, exploring your values, mapping your skills, auditing your network, envisioning your future self. Now comes the next part: staying in motion, in movementum.

This activity will help you design your next three months. It's not a rigid plan, but a winding path that keeps you moving, learning, and becoming.

You'll need: a journal or your computer nearby and about thirty to forty-five minutes to complete the activity.

Part 1: Celebrate Your Journey: Pause and Pat Yourself on the Back

Answer these four questions:

- Motivation: What matters to me and energizes me right now?
- Opportunities: What is already supporting me?
- Vision: Who I am becoming?
- Encouraging Community: Who is already supporting me?

In a journal, complete these prompts:

- As I look at all the activities I have done to date, what surprises me most is...
- The throughline I see connecting my past, present, and future is...
- What's calling me most strongly right now is...

Write for ten to fifteen minutes. Before you dig into what's next, pause and acknowledge what you've already discovered.

Part 2: Your Future Self

Now, imagine yourself three months from now. You've been actively exploring, experimenting, and in movementum.

Write this prompt in your journal:

- Three months from now, when I reflect on this period of my life, I will feel most fulfilled if I have...

Write freely for ten minutes. This is about what would genuinely bring you joy.

Now, read what you wrote and ask yourself:

- If I could focus on just one area for the next three months, one place where movement would feel the most meaningful—what would it be?

This focus is not a forever decision. It's simply the direction you're curious about right now.

My movementum focus for the next three months is:

____

This is a:

Mini move: Small, exploratory steps (trying something new, building a habit, testing an idea)

Mighty move: A bigger transition (changing roles, relocating, making a significant change)

Part 3: Design Your Path

Now you'll create three elements to support your move: a visual ritual, a rhythm for reflection, or experiments to try.

Your Visual Ritual

What image, object, or symbol will remind you of this journey?

My visual ritual is:

____

Your Rhythm for Reflection

Walking the bridge between current and future self requires regular check-ins. Not to judge yourself, but to notice: What am I learning? What's working? What wants to shift?

Choose a rhythm that feels sustainable (weekly or monthly), a time that's protected, and a place where you can think clearly.

My reflection ritual:

When: ______________________________________

(Example: Sunday evenings, first Monday of each month, Friday mornings)

Where: ______________________________________

(Example: my favorite coffee shop, my desk before anyone wakes up, on a walk)

What I'll reflect on:

- What brought me joy this week/month?
- What did I try that surprised me?
- What's one small adjustment I want to make?

Your Experiments

Experiments are how you explore the path. They're not commitments, they're curiosity driven. Some will work beautifully and others will reveal what you don't want. Either way, both are valuable.

Design two or three experiments you want to try in the next three months. Keep them small enough that they feel playful.

Experiment 1: Something I get to try this week

What I'll try: ______________________________

Why this interests me: ______________________________

What I might learn: ______________________________

Experiment 2: Something I'll Explore in Month 1–2

What I'll try: ______________________________

Why this interests me: ______________________________

What I might learn: ______________________________

Experiment 3: Something I'm Curious About for Month 2–3 (Optional)

What I'll try: ______________________________

Why this interests me: ______________________________

What I might learn: ______________________________

Your Fellow Traveler

Who will walk alongside you for these three months? This is about having someone who wants to see you thrive and check in on your journey.

Look back at your network review from chapter 9. Who comes to mind as someone who:

- Celebrates your wins without dimming them
- Asks good questions rather than giving advice

- Has your back
- Shows up consistently

My companion for this journey:

Name: ______________________________

Part 4: Review: One Step at a Time

The bridge from your current self to your future self starts with one small step. Not tomorrow but today. You've now completed a series of activities. Put a three-month reminder in place to come back to this book and answer:

- What brought me the most joy?
- What did I learn?
- What do I want to keep doing?
- What's my next focus?

Your Active Learning Path is a winding, surprising, sometimes challenging, often joyful journey. The destination matters less than staying in movementum. You're becoming that person right now, with each small step, each experiment, each moment of reflection.

The journey to your future self is not a solo tour. While there are aspects you'll want to navigate alone, much of this journey is most effective when you're surrounded by supportive people. The next chapter explores why community is the reinforcement that keeps your Active Learning Path strong and your movementum alive.

Key Points:

- **Move Along:** Your insights from the MOVE framework only create change when paired with structured action. The Active Learning Path is the bridge between knowing and doing.
- **Small Actions Create Movementum:** You don't need massive changes to move forward. Protecting small time pockets and maintaining simple rituals keep you in motion when life gets overwhelming.
- **Accelerate accountability:** Sharing intentions with an accountability partner and scheduling meetings dramatically increases follow-through.
- **There will be panic and potholes along the way:** It's a path that will be windy in parts. Stick to it. Now you have a backpack full of resources to help you stay the course.
- **Seldom solo:** While reflection requires solitude, lasting transformation happens with the help of community.

The next chapter explores why encouraging community is the final element that keeps your movementum alive.

PART V

ENCOURAGING COMMUNITY: CULTIVATING YOUR CIRCLE OF CONNECTIONS

Building support systems that sustain your journey

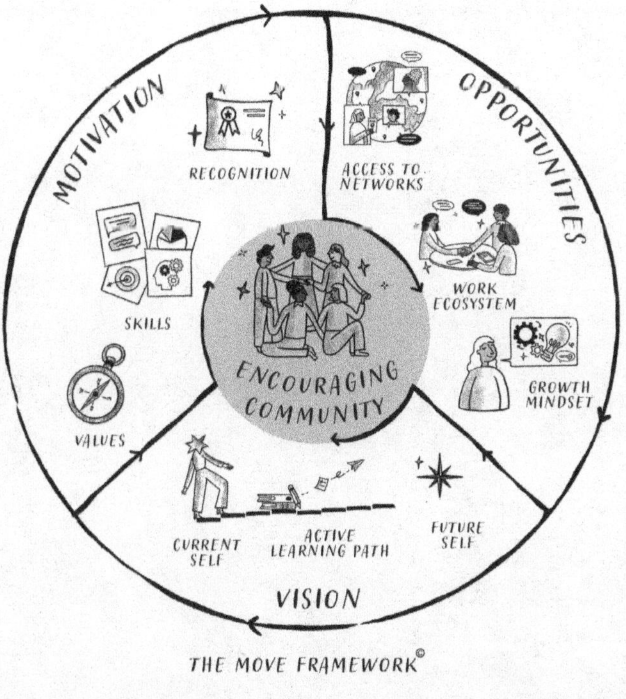

CHAPTER 16

NEVER GO IT ALONE: GROWING TOGETHER TO UPLIFT AND EMPOWER

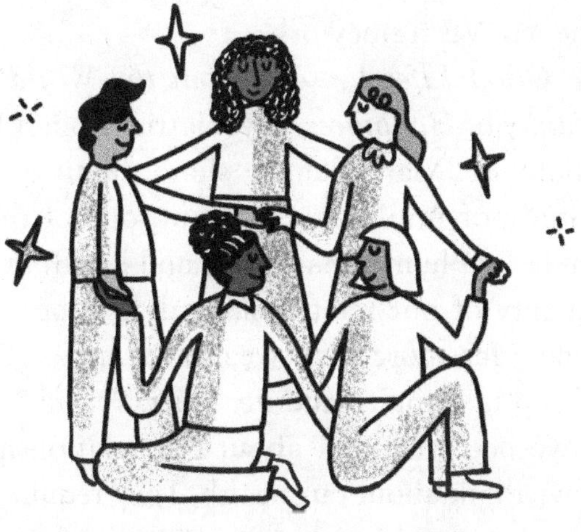

"Surround yourself with people who hand you back your dreams with encouragement."

—Anonymous

This is one of my favorite quotes because it captures what sustains lasting fulfillment, encouraging community. Your community may include childhood friends, family, colleagues, neighbors, or even familiar faces in your daily routines. What matters most is not who they are, but how they show up for you.

An encouraging community is a reflection of you. There's a saying: You're the average of the five people you spend the most time with.

Think about that: The people around you shape how you show up. Not only that but you need people who champion you as you are and keep you in movementum. Consider these people your marching band. That's what makes encouraging community the final, and perhaps most essential, piece of the MOVE framework.

In *The Good Life: Lessons from the World's Longest Scientific Study of Happiness,* psychiatrist Robert Waldinger and psychologist Marc Schulz share findings from the Harvard Study of Adult Development, one of the longest-running studies on human happiness and health. It spotlights that the quality of our relationships determines our health and happiness far more than wealth or fame. "Good relationships keep us happier and healthier. Period," Waldinger confirms. We need to think about our relationships in the same way we think about our health. They require intention, attention, and renewal for sustained fulfillment.

In fact, we see this principle in the world's longest-living communities, regions spanning Okinawa, Japan; Sardinia, Italy; Ikaria, Greece; Nicoya Peninsula, Costa Rica; and Loma Linda, California. Known as the Blue Zones, these communities thrive on deep social connections; they grow old in community with others, and prioritizing relationships is an essential part of their social infrastructure. They share meals, spend time together, and thrive in a system of mutual care. What sustains these communities is repeated connection.

But I also want to acknowledge that being in community can often be tough and not always a source of ease. Sometimes connection feels more like friction. You find yourself in energy-depleting relationships, navigating an irritating colleague, a family member you can't relate to, or an infuriating neighbor. Some relationships feel more like obligations than sources of support. Not everyone in your orbit will be a source of encouragement, some will drive you up the wall, others may be actively unhelpful. We aren't always able to choose who's a part of our communities, but being able to discern between the relationships that deserve your attention and those you keep at arm's length can give you peace of mind and help you find greater fulfillment.

WHEN COMMUNITY IS NOT YOUR CUP OF TEA

If you're reading this and thinking, "but community isn't for me," you're not alone. Not everyone needs an expansive social network. Some of us are energized by solitude and/or need significant recovery time after social interaction. However, studies show that some form of relational connection supports resilience and well-being, even when it's minimal or infrequent.

When encouraging community is absent, the effects can be felt quickly. Dr. Vivek Murthy, the former US surgeon general and author of *Together: The Healing Power of Human Connection in a Sometimes Lonely World,* talks about how loneliness severely decreases our quality of life. In fact, the health impact of loneliness is equivalent to smoking fifteen cigarettes a day!

In *Bowling Alone: The Collapse and Revival of American Community,* Harvard political scientist, Robert Putnam, documented the decline of community ever since television became a fixture in our lives. And now we also have social media to contend with, cannibalizing human interactions and making us feel emotionally connected to others while at a distance. We need human connection because it sustains us in ways that isolation cannot do.

But what is it about connection that we're craving? What makes certain relationships sustain us while others leave us feeling empty? The concept that captures what sits at the heart of an encouraging community is "mattering."

MATTERING: THE SOUL OF ENCOURAGING COMMUNITY

Journalist and author Jennifer Breheny Wallace explains in her book *Mattering: The Secret to a Life of Deep Connection and Purpose,* that mattering is a fundamental human need. Mattering is the experience of feeling valued by others coupled with the sense that one's actions add value to others. People who thrive have what Wallace calls a "mattering core"—an internal sense of feeling valued by family, friends, colleagues, and community, and knowing how they add value back. Wallace emphasizes that mattering is reciprocal. It's a two-way street: *feeling* valued and knowing that you *offer* value to others too. This is why mattering is essential to fulfillment. You can have all the work-life success, all the external markers of achievement, but without mattering, fulfillment remains elusive.

This connects directly to what we explored in Part II on motivation, where you explored living in alignment with your values, leveraging your skills, and understanding the importance of recognition. Mattering can only happen when you do work that lets your skills and values shine—and, this is key, others notice.

When those around you don't recognize your contributions it may be that they're busy or too worried about their own lives to see what you're doing. But it may also be that you're not letting others in, sharing your experiences so people can engage with you fully. Despite being more technologically connected than ever, most of us still feel disconnected. You may be in Slack channels with colleagues but feel invisible in meetings. You attend networking events but leave feeling more alone than when you arrived.

The struggle to feel like you matter is universal. It's even more pronounced for those experiencing bias and exclusion—where finding spaces where you genuinely matter becomes essential. Studies show that women of color, in particular, report lower levels of belonging and psychological safety at work, which makes access to communities where they genuinely feel seen and valued both harder to find and more essential for sustained work-life well-being.

Once you understand what it feels like to matter—and to make others feel they matter—you start to recognize how central it is to every meaningful community.

> **Once you understand what it feels like to matter-and to make others feel they matter-you start to recognize how central it is to every meaningful community.**

Mattering isn't confined to formal communities or networks. It's something to look for and create in all your interactions. When you do, you'll find that your relationships become richer and more fulfilling. And when your relationships are fulfilling, they make the journey worthwhile.

Understanding what mattering is, and why it's important, changes how you approach community building. You're not only looking for networking opportunities or social connections, you're looking for spaces where you can be fully yourself—and where you can help others do the same. And though not every community you encounter will support this, you *can* create the conditions for mattering to thrive in the communities you join and/or build.

CREATE CONDITIONS FOR MATTERING

You can be the one who instigates opportunities to connect. My friends who moved to the Hudson Valley and knew only a few people were over the moon to be invited to their neighbor's house, who started a regular coffee drop-in for the neighborhood. It forged connections beyond that polite wave from the car. Neighbors now rotate one weekend a month and host drop-in coffee meetups.

Priya Parker, in *The Art of Gathering*, reminds us that *how* we come together—with intention, purpose, and care—matters more than just showing up. She leads with the question: *Why* gather? That's a very relevant question to ask yourself before you choose to join any community: Why this one? Why now? What for? Don't expend your energy on lukewarm options.

Parker's research on gatherings highlights that strong communities are built through deliberate structure where boundaries, clear intentions, and meaningful participation create the conditions for people to feel they belong and that their presence matters. When gatherings are designed with this level of care, they become spaces of trust and connection—the foundations of any encouraging community.

Many years ago, when I was working for an international company, I attended a team-building cooking class. A chorus of complaints ensued the minute it was announced: "Do we have to stay the whole time? What if I don't like the cuisine? Why are we doing this?" And yet, as the evening unfolded, there was endless laughter and storytelling. This one event created deeper bonds and friendships among the team than months of working alongside each other ever could.

I call this the "social shuffle"—deliberately creating experiences where you can connect with different people in unexpected ways. Instead of always meeting the same friends for the same activities, mix it up: Visit a museum with a colleague, attend a lecture with someone from a different circle, explore a new neighborhood with acquaintances you'd like to know better. This is your Active Learning Path in action—experimenting with new ways of connecting and observing what works.

PAYING ATTENTION SIGNALS WHAT MATTERS

Wallace points out that distraction is a blocker to mattering, and I see this play out constantly. At events—even networking events designed for connection—I watch people lunge for their phones during breaks rather than turn to each other. This is the quiet unraveling of our ability to connect.

Of course, many of us need to check our devices. You might be waiting for word from a client or staying reachable for family emergencies. The issue isn't that you have your phone—it's whether you're using it intentionally or it's in charge of you. The message we send with distraction is clear: When you're scrolling while your colleague is talking, you're communicating that they don't matter enough to hold your attention. When you're checking notifications during a meeting, you're signaling that whatever might appear on your screen matters more than the people in the room. These behaviors directly impact how valued people feel in your presence.

Every time you get pulled into distraction, you're adding a hurdle to building connection. If you want to cultivate a meaningful community, you need to be present. This doesn't mean turning your devices off entirely—that's likely not realistic—but it does mean creating boundaries. Notifications are engineered to interrupt your thinking and pull you away—decide which ones truly require immediate attention and silence the rest. Practice leaving your phone in another room when not needed. The intention you put behind each decision determines whether you create a life where mattering—yours and others'—can take hold.

MATTERING IN ACTION

I have a friend, Betsy, who always sends handwritten thank-you cards. Specific ones that express how you made a difference and why it mattered. My friend Donna sends regular check-in texts just to see how I'm doing. These small gestures—they're heart warmers. They say without words: You matter to me. Small gestures with big impact will sustain you through the times you need them most. I'm sure you have come across small acts of kindness that moved you to tears. Why? Because it matters to us that we recognize each other. Be sure to not only find community but continue to actively create your own encouraging communities. Women I know describe their encouraging community as "my home team," "my safety network," "my unconditionally supportive pack of people."

For many people, in-person connection is not always possible. If that's the case for you, there are online communities that bring people together with the added benefit of reaching people from different countries and different circles you may not normally access. Virtual communities—whether through Zoom, Slack, WhatsApp groups, or online networks—can create genuine mattering when designed with intention. Mattering transforms a community from something you need to something that sustains you.

As you think about building your encouraging community, these questions can help you focus on what really matters:

- What does mattering mean to you?
- What's one invitation you could extend this week?
- What's one social experience you could create or participate in?
- How are you creating mattering for others in your life?

Your encouraging community exists to remind you that you're not alone—and that you matter. Not all communities are created equal, and knowing where to find the ones where mattering is at the heart of connection makes all the difference.

You might be wondering: Where do you find communities like this? Understanding how friendship markets work can help you know where to look.

THE FRIENDSHIP MARKET

Janice McCabe, a sociologist at Dartmouth College, has spent two decades studying friendship through a framework known as the "friendship market." A thriving friendship market exists when people in a particular setting are interested in making new friends, what McCabe describes as "buying" or "selling" friendship.

Most of the time you find yourself in weak friendship markets, where you don't need to make much effort because you already have established connections. This is evident, for example, when you show up to a work event but you already know everyone there. In these situations, McCabe explains, "intentionally putting yourself out there doesn't inspire reciprocation" because you're already part of the friend group.

But there are times when connection can feel hard. You're not part of the inner circle. The friendship market feels closed, as McCabe says. If you've shown up to networking events and felt like a wallflower, or joined groups where friendships seemed to form without you, it's likely a closed market. The good news is that once you understand this, you can be strategic about where you invest your energy.

So how do you find open friendship markets?

Open friendship markets tend to emerge during moments of transition. Whether you're changing roles, starting a business, becoming an empty nester, caring for aging parents, or experiencing any other shift, you're more likely to encounter others who are also re-evaluating who they are and how they want to live. These are often the spaces where encouraging community takes root.

This is where your KFC network from chapter 9 becomes relevant again: your knowledge holders, fans, and connectors. As you think about encouraging community, consider who you might need more of during this particular phase of your journey.

If you're looking for a new role in a different field or even within your current organization, knowledge holders may be helpful because they may offer practical wisdom and knowledge about your field of work; fans are ready to champion and cheer you on and your connectors may be poised to make introductions for you, opening doors to potential clients or collaborators you wouldn't have access to otherwise. Don't be discouraged if you don't have a full KFC bucket of connections. Whomever is currently most accessible to you is where you'll start, and maybe they can help you fill your other buckets. Community begets more community.

Research on how women learn and grow further reinforces the importance of community during times of change. In their book *Women's Ways of Knowing*, the authors Mary Field Belenky, Blythe McVicker Clinchy, Nancy

Rule Goldberger, and Jill Mattuck Tarule, found that women thrive in environments that promote "connected teaching," learning in relationship with others, through shared stories and experiences. We learn how to behave by observing ourselves as well as others, which explains why women's circles, clubs, and spaces continue to flourish. Women yearn for opportunities to connect, discover, learn from, and receive support from one another, creating the conditions for mattering that we explored earlier.

FINDING THE RIGHT COMMUNITY FOR YOU

In early 2026, Keta Bag, a community builder and LinkedIn creator, posted a simple question to her network: "What's the BEST women's community?" The response was overwhelming. Women from across industries and career stages flooded her inbox with recommendations—and not just names of communities, but heartfelt explanations of why these spaces mattered to them. Keta compiled the responses into a comprehensive spreadsheet, which she generously shares on her Substack, *Keta from Abroad*. The responses weren't just about professional advancement—they were about finding spaces where women could thrive and experience genuine fulfillment through connection.

The enthusiasm of the response to Keta's question reveals two things: how much women crave connection and community, and how varied those needs actually are. At any given point in your career or life, you'll navigate between different communities as what sustains you will change and your needs evolve. Early in your career, you might seek communities that offer access to jobs, mentors, or networks that open doors. Platforms like PowerToFly connect underrepresented talent with inclusive employers, while iFundWomen helps entrepreneurs raise capital and build businesses.

At other times in your life you may be exploring a new industry or role, which means you may need skills development through education-focused groups or technical training communities like Girls Who Code or Women Who Trade. You might seek inspiration and cross-industry connection through communities like CreativeMornings, a global creative community offering monthly talks and networking, both in cities worldwide and online. You might also prioritize visibility, learning, and professional growth, and seek to join communities like Luminary, a global professional networking and education platform for women and allies at all career stages, or platforms like Women Speakers Association, helping female speakers grow their visibility and income. There's also Black Girl Ventures, Latinas in Tech, The Mom Project for professionals seeking flexible work, or Society of Working Moms for women balancing careers and families.

In every space, you'll be looking for belonging where you need it most. Some communities are open to all; others are curated or invite-only. Some are free nonprofits; others require paid membership or investment commitments. Some meet in person; others operate entirely online.

> **In every space, you'll be looking for belonging where you need it most.**

Knowing what you need will help set you up for success with the communities most likely to move you forward. In a 2026 *New York Times* article entitled "Black Women Turn to Each Other as Their Career Paths Suddenly Recede," the author explained that with rising unemployment among Black professional women, many have started support groups via WhatsApp for help with resume writing, networking, and connecting. This is important because it shows that the fabric that binds us is still strong but that we miss the opportunity to nurture and strengthen these relationships on an ongoing basis, which might then make it easier to support each other in crisis.

Remember, building and maintaining your community takes patience, time, and energy. Don't wait until you desperately need a community to create one!

Here are some things to think about as you maintain your community:

Test It Out

Joining new communities can be exhilarating, but it can also be daunting if things don't pan out how you had planned. If you join an online community, for example, and the first gathering wasn't quite what you expected, you may need to give it another try. Give yourself a month or two before you bow out. Or maybe that specific community wasn't the right fit, but there's another that would be more closely aligned. As you're testing out different communities, ask yourself: Do I belong here? Do I matter here? Can I matter here? Belonging will get you in the door, but mattering is what will make you stay.

Initiate Gently

Encouraging community often grows through small signals of care. A brief message, a shared article, a note that says "this made me think of you" can strengthen connection without obligation. The CDC points out that "a few small acts of connection can build supportive, meaningful relationships." You don't need to wait to be invited in. Be the person "selling" your friendship on the open market. My husband, a voracious reader, is constantly sending articles to people he feels would find certain ideas informational or simply enjoyable—his community stretches far and wide, which has helped him strengthen work and social connections in his area of expertise. This may sound transactional, but just because someone can help you doesn't mean the relationship is purely utilitarian. Studies show that communities that share information and support each other are the healthiest.

Think in Layers

Your encouraging community is layered like a mille-feuille, a classic French pastry meaning "a thousand leaves," which traditionally features three layers of pastry and two layers of filling, topped with icing. It's decadent and delicious. Your community should be the same.

You have a layer that's your inner circle, the people who know you at your most vulnerable. They're the filling and consequently, the most essential part of your community. This filling is small as you cannot sustain deep relationships with a large number of people.

Then the next layer is your professional community: colleagues, mentors, industry peers, and acquaintances you have collected over the years. These relationships are in your periphery. This layer doesn't require the same intensity of connection as your inner circle, but it requires intentional care and follow-up, getting a coffee date in the calendar, dropping a brief text to check in.

And then there's the third layer, your everyday broader community: the person you chat with at the gym, the former colleague you see once a year, the neighbor you wave to on your commute to work, the people whose social media posts you like or comment on occasionally. These relationships might seem less important but they're touchpoints that remind us that your community is expansive. All three layers are essential because they offer different forms of connection of varying intensity. Sometimes, just waving to someone is going to be more than enough. On other days you might need a two-hour sit-down with your best friend. Your energy levels and circumstances ebb and flow, and your community needs to be flexible enough to meet you where you are. When you understand that your community operates in layers, you understand the value of each form of relationship.

Make It Micro

In order to rev up your community, try one-on-one coffee conversations rather than group gatherings. Or asynchronous online communities, like LinkedIn, may feel more sustainable than live events. Others prefer micro meetups with neighbors, baristas, or colleagues to feel a sense of belonging. Not every community is meant to last forever. Leaving one community is an opportunity to explore another.

All for One

Being in community underpins your fulfillment journey. When you share your wins with people who celebrate you, the wins expand. When you work through a setback, options and fresh perspectives can start to emerge. Encouraging communities function as a protective resource. They offer space for opportunity, buffer stress, and strengthen well-being, making it more feasible to pursue and sustain a fulfilling work life.

An acquaintance who made a work pivot reflected:

I had great people around me that helped. These safety networks helped me to overcome challenges and to find solutions because they were both advising me but also there for me emotionally when I was mentally drained.

Individuals who successfully navigate a work-life change don't do so in isolation. They actively leverage their networks of peers as sources of ideas, advice, and brainstorming. They reach out for counseling, inspiration, and reality checks. What makes the difference isn't just having a network. It's using community as a space to process experiences, test ideas, recalibrate, and gain perspective.

Everything you've worked on in this book—your motivations, your opportunities, your vision, your Active Learning Path—lives inside of you now. You're equipped for the trek ahead, and your encouraging community is here to ensure you don't need to carry the burdens alone.

The work life you're designing needs witnesses, cheerleaders, and truth tellers who hand you back your dreams with enthusiasm. Encouraging communities exist to remind you of who you're becoming and to help you move with steadiness and ease.

And at the heart of it all? Mattering—being valued and adding value in return.

Cultures around the world have understood that fulfillment comes through shared journeys. In South Africa, the philosophy of Ubuntu captures this beautifully: "I am because we are."

CHAPTER 17

BUILDING "MOVEMENTUM": STAYING ACTIVELY ENGAGED ON YOUR PATH TO FULFILLMENT

You've completed all four elements of the MOVE framework, but frameworks only work if you put them into practice. Let me bring you back to where we started.

Remember Zara?

When we met her in the introduction, she was nine months into her MBA, mulling over the promotion she'd been promised, feeling disappointed. She'd followed every rule—gotten the advanced degree, put in the hours, sacrificed weekends with her family—and still found herself unfulfilled, unmotivated, and on autopilot.

Eight months after that workshop, Zara sent me an email. The subject line read: "I did it."

She hadn't quit her job or moved to a new country or completely reinvented herself. Instead, she'd made what she called "a series of strategic pivots" within her sustainability company. She proposed a new green initiative that let her lead a cross-functional team. She negotiated to work remotely one day a week. She joined the board of a local environmental nonprofit, fulfilling her desire to develop new projects and be in the driver's seat again.

What changed wasn't her circumstances. It was Zara's relationship to her work life. She moved from passive recipient of her career choices to active architect of the work life she wanted.

That shift—from stuck to started—is what this book has been about.

You've done the work. You've identified your values, the skills that energize you, and the sources of recognition that matter. You've examined your work ecosystem and expanded your networks. You've envisioned your future self and designed an Active Learning Path to get there. You've built an encouraging community to sustain you along the way. The transformation isn't in completing the activities. It's in how you now see yourself and your relationship to your work life. It's in understanding how strategic moves create movementum.

> **The transformation is in understanding how strategic moves create movementum.**

So, what's next?

You'll have moments of clarity and moments of confusion. Breakthroughs and setbacks. Days when you feel deeply aligned with your values and wobbly days. My hope is that how you respond will be impacted by what you discovered between the covers of this book. Instead of doubling down on self-doubt or giving up entirely, you now have tools. You'll return to your values when you're feeling lost. You'll revisit your vision when you need direction. You'll reach out to your community when you need support. You'll talk to yourself with kindness instead of harsh criticism. And you'll keep moving.

Those who close their fulfillment gap don't have it all figured out nor do they move perfectly or without fear. They don't avoid all the potholes or panic moments, but they understand that clarity comes through action, and they believe that all types of moves lead to positive shifts. You won't get it right each time, but the point is to come back and reset.

Closing the fulfillment gap isn't just about getting a new job or a promotion or more money (though those might come too). It's about changing your relationship with yourself and your work life. It's claiming your right to want what you want and to move toward it with intention.

YOUR NEXT MOVE

Maybe you'll reach out to someone in your network. Maybe you'll propose a new project that uses your skills that thrill.

Maybe you'll block off twenty minutes for your first movementum ritual. Maybe you'll have that difficult conversation you've been avoiding.

Whatever it is, be sure to write it down and tell someone about it. Put it in your calendar.

That's how movementum begins: not with a massive overhaul, but with one intentional move at a time.

There will always be new desires, new challenges, new seasons that require recalibration, but the gap will narrow. You'll find pockets of joy and deep satisfaction even in the midst of hard seasons. You'll build a work life that reflects your values, leverages your strengths, and honors your whole self.

And that's what fulfillment actually is. Not the absence of challenges or the arrival at some perfect state but the deep satisfaction that comes from knowing you're actively shaping your life instead of passively accepting whatever comes your way. Zara is still at her company. She has hard days, of course, but she doesn't let them get her down. She's instilling the same principles in her daughter.

The work you do doesn't end here.

Consider joining forces with other communities of women and sharing what you're learning while navigating your own fulfillment journey. When someone takes their first brave step, be the encouragement they need. Your experience adds to our collective understanding of what it takes to close the fulfillment gap. I'd love to hear about your journey. Connect with me at hello@with-helen.com and let me know what moves you've made.

STAYING CONNECTED

Thank you for journeying through these pages with me.

Whether you picked up this book for yourself or to better support your team, I hope it has offered you fresh perspectives, practical tools, and the encouragement to create more fulfilling work—for yourself and those you lead.

For ongoing inspiration and practical insights, I invite you to subscribe to my Substack, where I share stories, frameworks, and thoughtful reflections on career fulfillment and leadership. Join a growing community of professionals redesigning their careers at **withhelen.substack.com**.

For additional resources, visit:

Here you'll find tools and materials to support your journey, including the frameworks in this book. **If you're looking to bring this work into your organization,** I partner with companies and leadership teams to create transformative experiences through:

- **Speaking engagements** on career advancement, leadership development, and workplace culture
- **Workshops and retreats** that inspire lasting growth and connection
- **Executive coaching** for individuals and teams ready to step into their next chapter

My sessions combine research-backed frameworks with warmth, authenticity, and practical tools that people can put into action immediately.

Planning to use this book with your team or book club? I'd love to support your journey and can even join your discussion. Interested in having me speak about the book at your event or on your podcast? Reach out directly at hello@with-helen.com

Let's also connect on LinkedIn, where I share insights and engage in meaningful conversations about careers and leadership at https://www.linkedin.com/in/helenkrugvonnidda/

Keep the movementum going. I'm cheering you on every step of the way.

With joy,
Helen

NOTES

INTRODUCTION: The Heart of the Journey

Author and neuroscientist Anne-Laure: Le Cunff, Anne-Laure. 2025. *Tiny Experiments: How to Live Freely in a Goal-Obsessed World.* Avery.

In their seminal book *Intrinsic Motivation:* Deci, Edward L., and Richard M. Ryan. 1996. *Intrinsic Motivation and Self-Determination in Human Behavior.* Plenum Press.

Even for those who haven't: Field, Emily, Alexis Krivkovich, Sandra Kügele, Nicole Robinson, and Lareina Yee. 2023. *Women in the workplace 2023.* McKinsey & Company.

Catalyst and Aspen Institute studies highlight: Catalyst. 1999. *Women of Color in Corporate Management: Opportunities and Barriers.* Catalyst.; Gallant, Erik. 2016. "For Women of Color, the Glass Ceiling Is Actually Made of Concrete." *Aspen Institute,* April 19. https://www.aspeninstitute.org/blog-posts/for-women-of-color-the-glass-ceiling-is-actually-made-of-concrete/.

Success and happiness have often been: Feenstra, Sanne, Christopher T. Begeny, Jennifer Jordan, Michelle K. Ryan, Janka I. Stoker, and Floor A. Rink. 2022. "Reaching the Top but Not Feeling on Top of the World: Examining Women's Internalized Power Threats." *Frontiers in Psychology 13* (December). https://doi.org/10.3389/fpsyg.2022.931314; Thompson Payton, L'Oreal. 2023. "53% of Women Say They're Lonely at Work and It

Only Gets Worse the Higher They Climb. Here's What Can Help." Yahoo! Finance, April 13. https://finance.yahoo.com/news/53-women-lonely-only-gets-090000972.html; Bareket, Orly, and Susan T. Fiske. 2025. "Lost Opportunities: How Gendered Arrangements Harm Men." *Proceedings of the National Academy of Sciences* 122 (5): e2320788122. https://doi.org/10.1073/pnas.2320788122.

A 2026 report by the Oliver Wyman Forum: Oliver Wyman Forum. 2026. *What 300,000 Voices Say About The Next Era Of Global Change.* https://www.oliverwymanforum.com/global-consumer-sentiment/300000-voices-next-era-global-change.html.

A number of personal-growth books: Blum, Beth. 2020. *The Self-Help Compulsion: Searching for Advice in Modern Literature.* Columbia University Press; Nehring, Daniel, Emmanuel Alvarado, Eric C. Hendriks, and Dylan Kerrigan. 2016. *Transnational Popular Psychology and the Global Self-Help Industry: The Politics of Contemporary Social Change.* Palgrave Macmillan.

Wall Street Journal **reporter and editor:** Bobrow, Emily. 2024. "Essay | Why Are Women Both Sadder and Happier Than Men?" Life. Wall Street Journal, March 22. https://www.wsj.com/lifestyle/relationships/why-arewomen-both-sadder-and-happier-than-men-4ffe1ba4.

Dr. Sonja Lyubomirsky's research: Lyubomirsky, Sonja. 2009. *The How of Happiness: A New Approach to Getting the Life You Want.* Penguin Books; Lyubomirsky, Sonja. 2014. *The Myths of Happiness: What Should Make You Happy, but Doesn't, What Shouldn't Make You Happy, but Does.* Penguin Books

PART I: "MINE" THE GAP: YOU ARE HERE

Chapter 1: The Fulfillment Gap: Understanding What's Missing

One prompt that I use regularly with clients: Boyatzis, Richard, Melvin L. Smith, and Ellen Van Oosten. 2019. *Helping People Change: Coaching with Compassion for Lifelong Learning and Growth*. Harvard Business Review Press.

In a *Harvard Business Review* article: Friedman, Stephen. 2024. "Your Career Doesn't Need to Have a Purpose." Career Planning. *Harvard Business Review,* April 23. https://hbr.org/2024/04/your-career-doesnt-need-to-have-a-purpose.

Yet, if everyone is having such a good time,: Chaker, Anne Marie. 2024. "Who's Happiest at Work? Hint: It's Not Women." Management. *Wall Street Journal,* May 6. https://www.wsj.com/lifestyle/careers/whos-happiest-at-work-hint-its-not-women-47932465.

***Fortune* magazine found that:** Belkin, Lisa. 2003. "The Opt-Out Revolution." Magazine. *The New York Times,* October 26. https://www.nytimes.com/2003/10/26/magazine/the-opt-out-revolution.html.

The concept of "squiggly careers,": Tupper, Helen, and Sarah Ellis. 2020. *The Squiggly Career: The No.1 Sunday Times Business Bestseller: Ditch the Ladder, Discover Opportunity, Design Your Career.* Portfolio Penguin.

Research finds that: Mainiero, Lisa A., and Sherry E. Sullivan. 2005. "Kaleidoscope Careers: An Alternate Explanation for the "opt-out" Revolution." *Academy of Management Perspectives 19* (1): 106–23. https://doi.org/10.5465/ame.2005.15841962; Mainiero, Lisa A., and Sherry E. Sullivan. 2006. *The Opt-out*

Revolt: Why People Are Leaving Companies to Create Kaleidoscope Careers. Nicholas Brealey.

In fact, there's a term for that feeling: Puspitasari, Ayu, and Miranti Putry. 2023. "The Sticky Floor Phenomenom a Literature Review." *Enrichment : Journal of Management 13* (3): 1813–21. https://doi.org/10.35335/enrichment.v13i3.1447.

A McKinsey & Company 2024 report highlights: McKinsey & Company, and LeanIn.Org. 2024. *Women in the Workplace 2024: The 10th-Anniversary Report*. McKinsey & Company; LeanIn.Org. https://www.mckinsey.com/featured-insights/diversity-and-inclusion/women-in-the-workplace-2024

Even when women: Catalyst. 2025. "Featured Research: Sponsorship & Mentorship." https://www.catalyst.org/insights/featured/sponsorship-mentoring.

Unsurprisingly, it's even worse: McKinsey & Company, and LeanIn.Org. 2024. *Women in the Workplace 2024: The 10th-Anniversary Report*. McKinsey & Company; LeanIn.Org. https://www.mckinsey.com/featured-insights/diversity-and-inclusion/women-in-the-workplace-2024

Research consistently shows that: Ehrlinger, Joyce, and David Dunning. 2003. "How Chronic Self-Views Influence (and Potentially Mislead) Estimates of Performance." *Journal of Personality and Social Psychology* (US) 84 (1): 5–17. https://doi.org/10.1037/0022-3514.84.1.5; Exley, Christine L., and Kirby Nielsen. 2024. "The Gender Gap in Confidence: Expected but Not Accounted For." *American Economic Review 114* (3): 851–85. https://doi.org/10.1257/aer.20221413; Hofer, Gabriela, Marla Hünninghaus, Jana Platzer, Sandra Grinschgl, and Aljoscha Neubauer. 2025. "Women's Humility and Men's Lack of Hubris: Gender Biases in Self-Estimated Spatial Intelligence." *Sex Roles 91* (4): 29. https://doi.org/10.1007/

s11199-025-01572-8; Kara-Yakoubian, Mane. 2025. "Women Underestimate Their Spatial Intelligence—Even When They Perform Just as Well as Men." *PsyPost: Psychology News*, May 6. https://www.psypost.org/women-underestimate-their-spatial-intelligence-even-when-they-perform-just-as-well-as-men/; Woodcock, Anna, William G. Graziano, Sara E. Branch, Ida Ngambeki, and Demetra Evangelou. 2012. "Engineering Students' Beliefs About Research: Sex Differences, Personality, and Career Plans." *Journal of Engineering Education* 101 (3): 495–511. https://doi.org/10.1002/j.2168-9830.2012.tb00059.x.

Countless studies back up this finding: Catalyst. 2024. "The Double-Bind Dilemma for Women in Leadership." February 16. https://www.catalyst.org/insights/2024/infographic-the-double-bind-dilemma-for-women-in-leadership; OECD. 2021. "Caregiving in Crisis: Gender Inequality in Paid and Unpaid Work during COVID-19." *OECD Policy Responses to Coronavirus (COVID-19)*, ahead of print, December 12. https://doi.org/10.1787/3555d164-en.

It doesn't help that a recent *Harvard Business Review* article: Waytz, Adam. 2023. "Beware a Culture of Busyness." Time Management. *Harvard Business Review*, March 1. https://hbr.org/2023/03/beware-a-culture-of-busyness.

In *Why We Can't Sleep*: Calhoun, Ada. 2021. *Why We Can't Sleep: Women's New Midlife Crisis*. Grove Press.

In *Rest Is Resistance*: Hersey, Tricia. 2022. *Rest Is Resistance: A Manifesto*. Little, Brown Spark

And Tiffany Dufu's *Drop the Ball* shows us: Dufu, Tiffany. 2018. *Drop the Ball: Achieving More by Doing Less*. Foreword by Gloria Steinem. Flatiron Books.

In their book, *Build the Life You Want:* Brooks, Arthur C., and Oprah Winfrey. 2023. *Build the Life You Want: The Art and Science of Getting Happier.* Portfolio

Research confirms that we tend to have: Baumeister, Roy F., Ellen Bratslavsky, Catrin Finkenauer, and Kathleen D. Vohs. 2001. "Bad Is Stronger than Good." *Review of General Psychology 5* (4): 323–70. https://doi.org/10.1037/1089-2680.5.4.323; Lazarus, John. 2021. "Negativity Bias: An Evolutionary Hypothesis and an Empirical Programme." *Learning and Motivation 75* (August): 101731. https://doi.org/10.1016/j.lmot.2021.101731; Watson, Joe, Sander van der Linden, Michael Watson, and David Stillwell. 2024. "Negative Online News Articles Are Shared More to Social Media." *Scientific Reports 14* (1): 21592. https://doi.org/10.1038/s41598-024-71263-z.

By creating more opportunities: Boyatzis, Richard, Melvin L. Smith, and Ellen Van Oosten. 2019. *Helping People Change: Coaching with Compassion for Lifelong Learning and Growth.* Harvard Business Review Press.

A number of cultures: Vikene, Odd, Frode Fretland, Suzanne Lundvall, and Petter Leirhaug. 2025. "Understandings of the Concept of Friluftsliv among Norwegian and International Students in a Changing World." *Journal of Adventure Education and Outdoor Learning,* September 3, 1–19. https://doi.org/10.1080/14729679.2025.2547231; Mautner, Raeleen D'Agostino. 2003. *Living La Dolce Vita: Italian Secrets to Living a Happy, Passionate, and Well-Balanced Life.* Sourcebooks.

But psychologist Dr. Tal Ben-Shahar's concept: Ben-Shahar, Tal. 2007. *Happier: Can You Learn to Be Happy?* McGraw Hill; Diener, Ed, Richard E. Lucas, and Christie Napa Scollon. 2006. "Beyond the Hedonic Treadmill: Revising the Adaptation

Theory of Well-Being." *American Psychologist* (US) 61 (4): 305–14. https://doi.org/10.1037/0003-066X.61.4.305.

Chapter 2: What We Can Learn from Thrivers

Similarly, Edina, a successful partner: Palmer, Parker J. 2000. *Let Your Life Speak: Listening for the Voice of Vocation By Parker J. Palmer.* Jossey-Bass.

PART II: MOTIVATION: PROPELLING YOU FORWARD

Chapter 4: Motivation: What Brings You Here?

Research shows that when you feel connected: Ryan, Richard M., and Edward L. Deci. 2000. "Self-Determination Theory and the Facilitation of Intrinsic Motivation, Social Development, and Well-Being." *American Psychologist* (US) 55 (1): 68–78. https://doi.org/10.1037/0003-066X.55.1.68; Weir, Kirsten. 2025. "Self-Determination Theory: A Quarter Century of Human Motivation Research." *American Psychological Association,* March 2. https://www.apa.org/research-practice/conduct-research/self-determination-theory; Pink, Daniel H. 2012. *Drive: The Surprising Truth About What Motivates Us.* Riverhead Books.

As Malcolm Gladwell, author of *Outliers:* Gladwell, Malcolm. 2011. *Outliers: The Story of Success.* Back Bay Books.

Chapter 5: Values: Exploring Your Core

As my good friend Sarah Young: Young, Sarah M. 2022. *Expansive Impact: An Invitation to Lead in Everyday Moments.* Amplify Publishing.

In one of our sessions she was: Brown, Brené. n.d. "Dare to Lead List of Values." *Brené Brown.* Accessed January 25, 2026. https://brenebrown.com/resources/dare-to-lead-list-of-values/.

Activity: Surfacing Your Values: Waldinger, Robert. 2025. "Building a Life of Wellness: The Science of Fostering Happiness and Health" Online Course. Module 2: Cultivating Values and Purpose.

Chapter 6: Skills: Harnessing Your Strengths

Research from Siri Terjesen: Terjesen, Siri. 2005. "Senior Women Managers' Transition to Entrepreneurship: Leveraging Embedded Career Capital." *Career Development International 10* (3): 246–59. https://doi.org/10.1108/13620430510598355.

Groundbreaking books like *What Color Is Your Parachute?*: Bolles, Richard N. 2022. *What Color Is Your Parachute?: Your Guide to a Lifetime of Meaningful Work and Career Success.* Ten Speed Press; Johnson, Spencer, and Kenneth Blanchard. 1998. *Who Moved My Cheese?: An A-Mazing Way to Deal with Change in Your Work and in Your Life.* G.P. Putnam's Sons.

Have you ever noticed…: Nakamura, Jeanne, and Mihaly Csikszentmihalyi. 2002. "The Concept of Flow." In *Handbook of Positive Psychology.* Oxford University Press.

In a seminal research study: Belenky, Mary Field, Blythe McVicker Clinchy, Nancy Rule Goldberger, and Jill Mattuck Tarule. 1997. *Women's Ways of Knowing (10th Anniversary Edition): The Development of Self, Voice, and Mind.* Basic Books.

But Gallup research suggests: Workhuman-Gallup Research Hub. 2024. *The Human-Centered Workplace: Building Organizational Cultures That Thrive.* Gallup-Workhuman. https://www.gallup.com/analytics/472658/workplace-recognition-research.aspx; Yi, Rachel. 2024. "Employee Retention Depends on

Getting Recognition Right." Gallup.Com, September 18. https://www.gallup.com/workplace/650174/employee-retention-depends-getting-recognition-right.aspx.

Chapter 7: Recognition: Acknowledging Your Value

I once watched a panel with Oprah: Tribeca, dir. 2017. *Tribeca TV Festival 2017 Oprah Shares What She Learned Hosting The Oprah Winfrey Show.* YouTube, September 23. https://www.youtube.com/watch?v=D6zUj1tKxiU.

A Gallup report from 2024: Workhuman-Gallup Research Hub. 2024. *The Human-Centered Workplace: Building Organizational Cultures That Thrive.* Gallup-Workhuman. https://www.gallup.com/analytics/472658/workplace-recognition-research.aspx; Yi, Rachel. 2024. "Employee Retention Depends on Getting Recognition Right." Gallup.Com, September 18. https://www.gallup.com/workplace/650174/employee-retention-depends-getting-recognition-right.aspx

Psychiatrist Anna Fels writes: Fels, Anna. 2013. *Necessary Dreams: Ambition in Women's Changing Lives.* Knopf Doubleday Publishing Group.

A 2023 Gallup study on recognition: Workhuman Gallup. 2023. *From Praise to Profits: The Business Case for Recognition at Work.* Workhuman. https://www.workhuman.com/resources/reports-guides/from-praise-to-profits-workhuman-gallup-report/?utm_source=businesswire&utm_medium=pr&utm_campaign=Q123_pr_NA&utm_content=release_gallup_32923; Business Wire. 2023. "New Workhuman-Gallup Study Finds Employee Recognition Can Help Businesses Gain Over $90 Million in Increased Productivity." Business Wire, March 29. https://www.businesswire.com/news/home/20230328005814/en/New-Workhuman-Gallup-Study-Finds-

Employee-Recognition-Can-Help-Businesses-Gain-Over-%2490-Million-in-Increased-Productivity.

In fact, research shows: Imran, Un Dini, Muhammad Faathir Ghazwan, and Firmansyah Firmansyah. 2025. "The Effect of Recognition and Appreciation on Employee Motivation and Performance." *Economics and Digital Business Review* 6 (1): 1-18. https://doi.org/10.37531/ecotal.v6i1.1890.

For women of color: Robotham, Kathrina. 2024. "Black Women Still Face a Glass Cliff, but Fixing Workplace Systems Can Change That." August 15. https://www.catalyst.org/insights/2024/black-women-glass-cliff-workplace-systems; Robotham, Kathrina, and Britney Jacobs. 2025. "Performance Feedback and Support Crucial for Retaining Black Employees." Catalyst, February 5. https://www.catalyst.org/insights/2025/retain-black-employees.

One movie that has stuck with me: Melfi, Theodore, dir. 2016. *Hidden Figures.* 20th Century Fox.

It wasn't until 2024: Atkinson, Joe. 2024. *NASA's Hidden Figures Honored with Congressional Gold Medals: NASA.* NASA.gov. Langley Research Center. September 19. https://www.nasa.gov/centers-and-facilities/langley/nasas-hidden-figures-honored-with-congressional-gold-medals/.

Stefanie Sword-Williams, author of *F*ck Being Humble*: Sword-Williams, Stefanie. 2020. *F*ck Being Humble.* Quadrille Publishing Ltd.

PART III: OPPORTUNITIES: MAXIMIZING MOMENTS

Chapter 8: Optimizing Opportunities

Mark Granovetter, a social scientist and professor: Granovetter, Mark. 1983. "The Strength of Weak Ties: A Network Theory Revisited." *Sociological Theory 1*: 201–33. https://doi.org/10.2307/202051.

Chapter 9: Accessing Your Networks

In her book, *Build Like a Woman:* Griffith, Kathleen. 2024. *Build Like a Woman: The Blueprint for Creating a Business and Life You Love.* St. Martin's Essentials.

As Minda Harts reminds us: Harts, Minda. 2019. *The Memo: What Women of Color Need to Know to Secure a Seat at the Table.* Seal Press.

A number of studies show: Waldinger, Robert, and Marc Schulz. 2023. *The Good Life: Lessons from the World's Longest Scientific Study of Happiness.* Simon & Schuster; Cambieri, Giulia. 2024. *The Importance of Connections: Ways to Live a Longer, Healthier Life.* December 8. https://hsph.harvard.edu/news/the-importance-of-connections-ways-to-live-a-longer-healthier-life/; Holt-Lunstad, Julianne. 2024. "Social Connection as a Critical Factor for Mental and Physical Health: Evidence, Trends, Challenges, and Future Implications." *World Psychiatry 23* (3): 312–32. https://doi.org/10.1002/wps.21224.

In *The Lost Art of Connecting*, Susan McPherson: McPherson, Susan, and Jackie Ashton. 2021. *The Lost Art of Connecting: The Gather, Ask, Do Method for Building Meaningful Business Relationships.* McGraw Hill.

And it's not just: Granovetter, Mark. 1983. "The Strength of Weak Ties: A Network Theory Revisited." *Sociological Theory* 1: 201–33. https://doi.org/10.2307/202051.

As Keith Ferrazzi, author of *Never Eat Alone:* Ferrazzi, Keith, and Tahl Raz. 2014. *Never Eat Alone, Expanded and Updated: And Other Secrets to Success, One Relationship at a Time.* Crown Currency.

In her book *Strategize to Win:* Harris, Carla A. 2014. *Strategize to Win: The New Way to Start Out, Step Up, or Start Over in Your Career.* Avery.

Research shows that similarity breeds connection: McPherson, Miller, Lynn Smith-Lovin, and James M. Cook. 2001. "Birds of a Feather: Homophily in Social Networks." *Annual Review of Sociology 27* (Volume 27, 2001): 415–44. https://doi.org/10.1146/annurev.soc.27.1.415; McKinsey & Company, and LeanIn.Org. 2025. *Women in the Workplace 2025: The Annual Report.* McKinsey & Company; LeanIn.Org. https://www.leanin.org/women-in-the-workplace

Women of color lack: McKinsey & Company, and LeanIn.Org. 2025. *Women in the Workplace 2025: The Annual Report.* McKinsey & Company; LeanIn.Org. https://www.leanin.org/women-in-the-workplace.[CH1]

Research by Herminia Ibarra: Ibarra, Herminia. 1992. "Homophily and Differential Returns: Sex Differences in Network Structure and Access in an Advertising Firm." *Administrative Science Quarterly* 37 (3): 422–47.

For women specifically: Rua-Gomez, Carla, Gianluca Carnabuci, and Martin Goossen. 2022. "Reaching for the Stars: How Gender Influences the Formation of High-Status Collaboration Ties." *Academy of Management Journal* 66 (August). https://doi.org/10.5465/amj.2021.0218.

Chapter 10: Work Ecosystem: Optimizing Your Workplace Dynamics

National Geographic defines the ecosystem: National Geographic Education. n.d. "Ecosystem." Accessed January 24, 2026. https://education.nationalgeographic.org/resource/ecosystem.

As Dr. Ella F. Washington reminds us: Washington, Ella F. 2024. *Unspoken: A Guide to Cracking the Hidden Corporate Code.* Forbes Books.

It doesn't help that Harvard Business School: DeFilippis, Evan, Stephen Michael Impink, Madison Singell, Jeffrey T. Polzer, and Raffaella Sadun. 2020. *Collaborating During Coronavirus: The Impact of COVID-19 on the Nature of Work.* No. W27612. National Bureau of Economic Research. https://doi.org/10.3386/w27612; Kost, Danielle. 2020. "You're Right! You Are Working Longer and Attending More Meetings." Harvard Business School's Working Knowledge: Distilling Harvard Business School Research for Leaders Who Make a Difference, September 14. https://www.library.hbs.edu/working-knowledge/you-re-right-you-are-working-longer-and-attending-more-meetings.

Chapter 11: Your Mindset Is Your Greatest Asset

Psychologist Carol Dweck calls this: Dweck, Carol S. 2006. *Mindset: The New Psychology of Success.* Ballantine Books.

As psychologist Rick Hanson explains: Hanson, Rick. 2010. "Taking In The Good: Do Positive Experiences 'Stick to Your Ribs?'" Psychology Today, February 6. https://www.psychologytoday.com/us/blog/your-wise-brain/201002/taking-in-the-good.

Tara Mohr, author of *Playing Big:* Mohr, Tara. 2015. *Playing Big: Practical Wisdom for Women Who Want to Speak Up, Create, and Lead.* Avery.

Shirzad Chamine, in his work on *Positive Intelligence:* Chamine, Shirzad. 2016. *Positive Intelligence: Why Only 20% of Teams and Individuals Achieve Their True Potential and How You Can Achieve Yours.* Greenleaf Book Group Press.

PART IV: VISION: WHERE DO YOU SEE YOURSELF?

Chapter 12: Personal Vision

Career development research shows: Schlossberg, Nancy K., Elinor B. Waters, and Jane Goodman. 1995. *Counseling Adults in Transition: Linking Practice with Theory.* Springer Publishing Company.

Studies reveal that women who develop: Buse, Kathleen R., and Diana Bilimoria. 2014. "Personal Vision: Enhancing Work Engagement and the Retention of Women in the Engineering Profession." *Frontiers in Psychology* 5 (December). https://doi.org/10.3389/fpsyg.2014.01400.

Chapter 13: Current Self: Who Am I?

Psychologist Dan McAdams's work on narrative identity: McAdams, Dan P. 1997. *The Stories We Live By: Personal Myths and the Making of the Self.* The Guilford Press; McAdams, Dan P., and Kate C. McLean. 2013. "Narrative Identity." *Current Directions in Psychological Science* 22 (3): 233–38. https://doi.org/10.1177/0963721413475622.

As Danish philosopher Søren Kierkegaard wrote: Kierkegaard, Søren. 2007. *Soren Kierkegaard's Journals and Notebooks, Vol. 1: Journals AA-DD*. Edited by Bruce H. Kirmmse, Niels Jørgen Cappelørn, Alastair Hannay, George Pattison, and Jon Stewart. Princeton University Press.

Psychologist E. Tory Higgins: Higgins, E. Tory. 1987. "Self-Discrepancy: A Theory Relating Self and Affect." *Psychological Review* (US) 94 (3): 319–40. https://doi.org/10.1037/0033-295X.94.3.319.

Research on human agency: Ryan, Richard M., and Edward L. Deci. 2000. "Self-Determination Theory and the Facilitation of Intrinsic Motivation, Social Development, and Well-Being." *American Psychologist* (US) 55 (1): 68–78. https://doi.org/10.1037/0003-066X.55.1.68; Masten, Ann S. 2001. "Ordinary Magic: Resilience Processes in Development." *American Psychologist* (US) 56 (3): 227–38. https://doi.org/10.1037/0003-066X.56.3.227.

Psychologist Albert Bandura: Bandura, Albert. 1997. *Self-Efficacy: The Exercise of Control.* Self-Efficacy: The Exercise of Control. W H Freeman/Times Books/Henry Holt & Co.

In fact, psychologist Martin Seligman: Seligman, Martin E. P. 2011. *Learned Optimism: How to Change Your Mind and Your Life.* Vintage; Peterson, Christopher, Martin E. Seligman, and George E. Vaillant. 1988. "Pessimistic Explanatory Style Is a Risk Factor for Physical Illness: A Thirty-Five-Year Longitudinal Study." *Journal of Personality and Social Psychology* (US) 55 (1): 23–27. https://doi.org/10.1037/0022-3514.55.1.23.

This matters because: Sword-Williams, Stefanie. 2026. *Career Comedown: What to Do When Work Isn't Working for You.* Fourth Estate.

Chapter 14: Becoming You: Your Future Self

Peter Senge, MIT professor and author: Senge, Peter M. 2006. *The Fifth Discipline: The Art & Practice of The Learning Organization.* Doubleday.

Athletes like Gabby Thomas and Coco Gauff: Hoffman, Kelsie. 2024. "Gabby Thomas on Winning Gold at 2024 Paris Olympics: 'I Knew I Was Ready for That Moment': CBS News." Cbsnews.Com, August 13. https://www.cbsnews.com/news/gabby-thomas-talks-preparing-for-2024-paris-games-winning-first-ever-olympic-gold-medal/; Pugmire, Jerome. 2025. "Coco Gauff Used Words and a Mirror to Persuade Herself She Could Win the French Open—Boston Herald." Boston Herald. Accessed January 24, 2026.

Dr. Boyatzis's research on the ideal self shows: Boyatzis, Richard E., and Kleio Akrivou. 2006. "The Ideal Self as the Driver of Intentional Change." *Journal of Management Development 25* (7): 624–42. https://doi.org/10.1108/02621710610678454; Boyatzis, Richard, Melvin L. Smith, and Ellen Van Oosten. 2019. *Helping People Change: Coaching with Compassion for Lifelong Learning and Growth.* Harvard Business Review Press.

For the neuroscience showing brain activation when envisioning the ideal self, see Jack, Anthony I., Richard E. Boyatzis, Masud S. Khawaja, Angela M. Passarelli, and Regina L. Leckie. 2013. "Visioning in the Brain: An fMRI Study of Inspirational Coaching and Mentoring." *Social Neuroscience 8* (4): 369–84. https://doi.org/10.1080/17470919.2013.808259.

UCLA psychologist Hal Hershfield's: Ersner-Hershfield, Hal, G. Elliott Wimmer, and Brian Knutson. 2009. "Saving for the Future Self: Neural Measures of Future Self-Continuity Predict Temporal Discounting." *Social Cognitive and Affective*

Neuroscience 4 (1): 85–92. https://doi.org/10.1093/scan/nsn042.

Herminia Ibarra, whom I mentioned in chapter 9: Ibarra, Herminia. 1992. "Homophily and Differential Returns: Sex Differences in Network Structure and Access in an Advertising Firm." *Administrative Science Quarterly 37* (3): 422–47.

As psychologist Gay Hendricks mentions: Hendricks, Gay. 2010. *The Big Leap: Conquer Your Hidden Fear and Take Life to the Next Level⊠A Transformative Guide to Overcoming Fears and False Beliefs for Personal Growth and Success.* HarperOne.

Chapter 15: Your Active Learning Path

Dr. John Ratey's research in *Spark:* Hagerman, Eric, and John J. Ratey MD. 2013. *Spark: The Revolutionary New Science of Exercise and the Brain.* Little, Brown Spark.

Across studies of behavior change: Faries, Mark D. 2016. "Why We Don't 'Just Do It.'" *American Journal of Lifestyle Medicine 10* (5): 322–29. https://doi.org/10.1177/1559827616638017.

According to neuroscientist Anne-Laure: Le Cunff, Anne-Laure. 2025. *Tiny Experiments: How to Live Freely in a Goal-Obsessed World.* Avery.

Georgia O'Keeffe took a daily: Currey, Mason, ed. 2013. *Daily Rituals: How Artists Work.* Knopf.

Leonard Cohen developed a pre-performance ritual: Bray, Elisa. 2012. "Leonard Cohen: Before the Gig, a Chant in Latin." The Independent, September 6. https://www.the-independent.com/arts-entertainment/music/features/leonard-cohen-before-the-gig-a-chant-in-latin-8104872.html.

Marshall Goldsmith, author and executive coach: Goldsmith, Marshall, and Mark Reiter. 2007. *What Got You Here Won't Get You There: How Successful People Become Even More Successful.* Grand Central Publishing.

Seth Godin, bestselling author of *Tribes: We Need You to Lead Us:* Godin, Seth. 2024. "Why Everything You Know About Success & Productivity Is Wrong." Interview by Marie Forleo. MarieTV, October 29. https://www.marieforleo.com/blog/seth-godin-success.

Psychologist Ethan Kross's research: Kross, Ethan. 2021. *Chatter: The Voice in Our Head, Why It Matters, and How to Harness It.* Crown; Kross, Ethan, Emma Bruehlman-Senecal, Jiyoung Park, et al. 2014. "Self-Talk as a Regulatory Mechanism: How You Do It Matters." *Journal of Personality and Social Psychology 106* (2): 304–24. https://doi.org/10.1037/a0035173.

In a study by researchers Rachel White: White, Rachel E., Emily O. Prager, Catherine Schaefer, Ethan Kross, Angela L. Duckworth, and Stephanie M. Carlson. 2017. "The 'Batman Effect': Improving Perseverance in Young Children." *Child Development 88* (5): 1563–71. https://doi.org/10.1111/cdev.12695.

PART V: ENCOURAGING COMMUNITY: CULTIVATING YOUR CIRCLE OF CONNECTIONS

Chapter 16: Never Go It Alone: Growing Together to Uplift and Empower

In *The Good Life:* Waldinger, Robert, and Marc Schulz. 2023. *The Good Life: Lessons from the World's Longest Scientific Study of Happiness.* Simon & Schuster.

In fact, we see this principle: Buettner, Dan. 2012. *The Blue Zones, Second Edition: 9 Lessons for Living Longer from the People Who've Lived the Longest.* Disney Hyperion Digital.

Dr. Vivek Murthy, the former US surgeon general: Murthy, Vivek H. 2023. *Together: The Healing Power of Human Connection in a Sometimes Lonely World.* Harper Paperbacks.

In *Bowling Alone:* Putnam, Robert D. 2020. *Bowling Alone: Revised and Updated: The Collapse and Revival of American Community.* Simon & Schuster.

Journalist and author Jennifer Breheny Wallace: Wallace, Jennifer Breheny. 2023. *Never Enough: When Achievement Culture Becomes Toxic-and What We Can Do About It.* Portfolio.

Studies show that women of color: McKinsey & Company, and LeanIn.Org. 2022. *Women in the Workplace 2022: Annual Report.* McKinsey & Company; LeanIn.Org. Accessed January 30, 2026. https://womenintheworkplace.com/2022; Jolly, Jallicia. 2025. "Beyond Glass Ceilings And Glass Cliffs, Black Women Professors In Higher Education Offer Leadership Lessons." Forbes, January 24. https://www.forbes.com/sites/jalliciajolly/2026/01/24/beyond-glass-ceilings-and-glass-cliffs-black-women-professors-in-higher-education-offer-leadership-lessons/.

Priya Parker, in *The Art of Gathering:* Parker, Priya. 2020. The Art of Gathering: How We Meet and Why It Matters. Riverhead Books.

Janice McCabe, a sociologist: McCabe, Janice. 2026. "Opinion | I Study Friendship. Here's How You Make Lasting Friends." Opinion. *The New York Times,* January 3. https://www.nytimes.com/2026/01/03/opinion/friendship-markets-new-friends.html

In their book *Women's Ways of Knowing:* Belenky, Mary Field, Blythe McVicker Clinchy, Nancy Rule Goldberger, and Jill Mattuck Tarule. 1997. *Women's Ways of Knowing (10th Anniversary Edition): The Development of Self, Voice, and Mind.* Basic Books.

In early 2026, Keta Bag: See https://ketabag.substack.com/ for ongoing list of communities.

In a 2026 *New York Times:* Holman, Jordyn. 2026. "Black Women Turn to One Another as Their Career Paths Suddenly Recede." Business. *The New York Times,* January 17. https://www.nytimes.com/2026/01/17/business/black-women-job-market-hiring-careers-dei.html.

The CDC points out: CDC. 2025. "Improving Social Connectedness." Social Connection, February 5. https://www.cdc.gov/social-connectedness/improving/index.html.

Studies show that communities: Holt-Lunstad, Julianne. 2024. "Social Connection as a Critical Factor for Mental and Physical Health: Evidence, Trends, Challenges, and Future Implications." World Psychiatry 23 (3): 312–32. https://doi.org/10.1002/wps.21224; Moldavanova, Alisa V., Dorothy M. Daley, and John C. Pierce. 2025. "What Does It Take to Have a Healthy Community? Exploring the Role of Social Infrastructure in Shaping Public Health." *The American Review of Public Administration 55* (5): 396–414. https://doi.org/10.1177/02750740251346805; World Health Organization. 2025. From Loneliness to Social Connection: Charting a Path to Healthier Societies. Geneva. https://www.who.int/publications/i/item/978240112360.

ACKNOWLEDGMENTS

Woohoo! I am thrilled to celebrate my very own encouraging community—the people who made this book possible and cheered me on along the way.

Ruthie Ackerman, there are not enough characters on a keyboard to express my joy at having you as my editor, book coach, mentor, writing whisperer, and unwavering champion. You are the most stylish fairy godmother of the written page. Thank you for the hand-holding, the patience with my hand-wringing, and for believing in this book from the very beginning. We did it!

My agents at Aevitas, Jane von Mehren and Donya Dickerson. How lucky was I to have you take me under your wing? Jane, your steadiness, wisdom, and warmth carried me through this process. Donya, your intuition and kindness know no bounds. I am deeply grateful you took a chance on me.

My team at Post Hill Press, Debby Englander and Lauren Campbell, your enthusiasm and care in embracing this book have been wonderful. It has been a joy to work with you.

To the women who participated in my doctoral research and in my programs and events—hearing your stories, witnessing your growth, and learning from you is the reason I do this work. This book exists because of you. To my coaching clients, thank you for your trust and partnership. Our work together has been a constant source of learning and inspiration.

TO MY COLLABORATORS:

Liza Summers, working with you on with-helen.com over the years has been such a joy. You have an extraordinary ability to see the heart of my work and help shape how its story is told. Thank you for your constant positivity and encouragement.

Mina Yanci Ibis, you are such a gifted illustrator, and you captured the spirit of this book beautifully. Thank you for bringing my work to life with joy and originality.

Dr. Charity Hoffman, I'm so grateful for your thoughtful and brilliant collaboration in this research.

Dorie Clark, Anne-Laure Le Cunff, Alim Dhanji, Brian Baker, Dr. Ruth Gotian, Fran Hauser, Deepa Purushothaman, Amy Shoenthal, Terri Trespicio and Dr. Ella Washington, your thought leadership continues to inspire and guide me.

Sarah Young, our voice mails were a lifeline throughout this journey. Thank you for every down-to-earth exchange and for keeping it real for me throughout with such humor.

Cate Luzio, your vision in building Luminary has been remarkable. I'm deeply grateful you've always invited me to share my work in this beautiful community.

Maria Schmitt, your generosity of spirit in our coaching and course design together deepened my work in countless ways. It is a gift to call you a dear friend.

Abi Green, thank you for your creativity and imagination in helping MOVE take new forms. Our collaboration has been truly special.

Stephen Morrison, I am so grateful for the richness of your insights and guidance as I explored writing this book.

Roger Jones, thank you for the early brainstorming sessions that helped refine my research into an actionable framework.

TO MY CIRCLE OF FRIENDS, YOU ARE MY CONFETTI IN A CUP:

Lisa (Jaaackson), we knew in primary school that we would be forever friends. Our adventures have filled my heart and made for endless belly laughs, and being godmother to your perfect son, Alex, has been one of my greatest honors.

Claire (Wellyboot) and Flora (La Flo), *mes sœurs de la vie,* my sisters in all the ways that matter. We will never run out of stories that make us hoot and holler.

Betsy (La Boob), you championed my dream when I said I wanted to live in New York. And here we are. Your energy and love are unparalleled.

Monica (Mo), you're the link to all good things, connecting people to possibilities and making things happen. You sprang into action the moment I said I was looking to write a book, jump-starting this adventure. You are not only the best, you also bust a move.

Brett and Jacob, thank you for being trusted sounding boards on this book and for being wonderful friends.

And to Kay (Tart), Donna (Doner), Elizabeth (Elizubeth), Sabine (Beanie), Allison (Cricket), Tracy (Lady O), Aliya (hey gurl hey), Anne M. (Nouchette), Ingrid (Poulette), Anne F. (Copinette), Sani (DZek), John (Wonny), Dalila—and to those whose names I could not fit on this page—please know my heart is full to the brim with love for you. You always show up with generosity and unwavering support.

TO MY TEACHERS AND PEERS:

My theatre professors at Smith College—Andrea Hairston, Deborah Lubar, Kiki Smith—thank you for teaching me to trust my voice and amplify it boldly.

Dr. Victoria Marsick, Dr. Lyle Yorks, Dr. Jeanne Bitterman, Teachers College, Columbia University, where this research began and where I found my home, thank you for providing the academic grounding for this work. And above all, Dr. Marie Volpe, my doctoral advisor—your love and wisdom guided me through every step.

Sam House and Carey Baker of the Co-Active Training Institute, thank you for your deeply formative approach to coaching. Your work shaped my path and continues to inform how I practice, teach, and lead.

My former HR colleagues and now firm friends: my one and only forever upbeat Leni, Michael D., Arturo, Nina, Mehmet, and Veronique. Our work together sparked what I poured into these pages.

TO MY FAMILY:

To my late grandmother Lillibelle, who remains deeply present in my heart. To my aunt Madge, whose passion for learning reminds me that growth is a lifelong practice.

To Monique M.—your home was where I first learned what it meant to be part of an encouraging community, and it remains among my most cherished childhood memories.

To my extraordinary mum, Sybil (Mutti), you never cease to amaze me with the journey you took to build the life you envisioned for me. You moved heaven and earth to give me the ground from which to soar. Thank you for teaching me to live from the heart, to follow my many dreams, and above all, to laugh often.

To Bee, my formidable husband and one-man marching band. You are my rock (and roll). It continues to be a joy to discover this funny thing called life with you. You believe in me every single day. Your brilliance and your enthusiasm are unmatched, as is your talent for cocktail making, snacks, meals, and music mixing. I am in awe of who you continue to become and am so very proud to walk and dance beside you every day.

And finally, to New York City. You make my heart sing.

ABOUT THE AUTHOR

Photo credit: David Noles

Dr. Helen Krug von Nidda is an executive coach, international speaker, and educator specializing in leadership transformation and career empowerment with a focus on professional women.

With over twenty years of global HR experience, she has worked with organizations including Morgan Stanley, Sony Music, L'Oréal, Dell, and the United Nations. Her work includes facilitating team engagements, delivering leadership workshops, and leading coaching programs for Fortune 500 companies, global nonprofits, and international organizations. Helen is an instructor at Stanford University, Columbia University, and Smith College. She has also served as an executive coach at IMD Business School in Switzerland and INSEAD in France. She holds a Doctorate in Education from Columbia University, an MA from Webster University, a BA from Smith College, and is a certified coach and licensed career counselor.

Born in London, raised in Switzerland, and educated in the United States, her work has been featured in *Forbes* and *Fast Company*. She currently lives in Manhattan with her husband. She enjoys her daily hot chocolate and morning jogs along the Hudson River.